EUTHANASIA AND RELIGION

EUTHANASIA
AND
RELIGION

ૐ

A survey of the attitudes
of world religions
to the right-to-die

ૐ

GERALD A. LARUE

THE HEMLOCK SOCIETY
LOS ANGELES

A paperback original
First published, 1985
Reprinted, 1986

Library of Congress Number: 84-62806
ISBN 0-394-62078X   E996
Distributed by: Grove Press Inc.
196 W. Houston St., NY, NY 10014

Published in the USA by
The Hemlock Society
PO Box 66218
Los Angeles, CA 90066

Contents

About the Author

Dr. Gerald A. Larue, President of the Hemlock Society, is Emeritus Professor of Religion and Adjunct Professor of Gerontology at the University of Southern California. He is a member of the prestigious Academy of Humanism, author of a number of books including *Ancient Myth and Modern Man* (Prentice-Hall) and *Sex and the Bible* (Prometheus), and his articles appear regularly in *Free Inquiry* magazine and other national publications. He is Leader of the Ethical Culture Society of Los Angeles, and a Marriage, Family Child therapist with The Taylor Therapy Center in Beverly Hills where he specializes in cases involving death, grief, loss, attempted suicide and related issues.

Preface

There were at least three reasons for undertaking this survey of religious attitudes to euthanasia. First, with my colleague Dr. James. A. Peterson, I teach a class entitled "Social and Psychological Aspects of Death and Dying" at the University of Southern California. Inevitably, when we come to the section on euthanasia, religious beliefs are involved. We both realized that we needed more information on this important aspect of the subject. Second, I was invited to present a paper on this theme at the international meeting of The World Federation of Right to Die Societies, held in Nice, France, in 1984. I was a member of the Board of Directors of this organization from 1980–84. Third, as President of the Hemlock Society and at the prompting of its Director, Derek Humphry, I was persuaded that the Society needed more information about religious attitudes on euthanasia.

Thanks to Dr. David Peterson, Director of the Leonard Davis School of Gerontology (where I teach), I was permitted to use the university mailing address. Paper, postage, and printing costs were underwritten by Hemlock. Emily Perkins, a member of Hemlock's Board of Directors, assisted greatly in organizing the project.

I am grateful to the clergy who responded so graciously to my questionnaire and who directed me to reference materials and to persons who could be of help in their respective denominations. Of course there were those who did not respond or who simply wrote a single comment on the question sheet. Because of pressures of time and another research project, my findings were limited to what was available during the allotted period.

For several years, a far more comprehensive research program, "Project Ten," has been sponsored by the Lutheran General Medical Conference. It has been described as a multi-year, multidisciplinary study, called *Health/Medicine, and Faith Traditions*. The project seeks to understand how philosophical, theological, and pastoral resources of religious traditions apply and respond to life and death concerns of health and medicine. More than twenty faiths are represented; top scholars, theologians, pastors, ethicists, and clinical practitioners are involved. Some items have already been published in *Health/Medicine and the Faith Traditions: An Inquiry into Religion and Medicine* (Martin Marty and Kenneth Vaux, eds., Fortress Press, 1983). Such studies go far beyond this present survey and provide in-depth understanding of the relationship of belief systems to the broad issues of life, dying, and death.

My inquiry is limited to the questions presented in the questionnaire, a copy of which appears in the Appendix—and the focus is solely on euthanasia. In addition to the answers provided in responses to the questionnaire, articles in denominational periodicals and in journals of religion have also been consulted. Some of these are utilized in the discussion of specific denominational attitudes, and many are listed in the Bibliography.

Gerald A. Larue
Emeritus Professor, Religion
Adjunct Professor, Gerontology
The University of Southern California

Euthanasia and Religion

Introduction

There is some risk in surveying the opinions of religious leaders and officials, just as there is in taking opinion polls of religious beliefs in general. In the United States of America, Harris polls, Gallup polls, and a variety of other surveys reflect popular opinions and attitudes. To ask, as I have done, "Does your religious organization believe in an afterlife?" may save space and almost invite the response, "Organizations don't hold particular beliefs, people do . . . ," but the question in and of itself doesn't really demonstrate much.

A wider sampling might includes questions about belief in punishment in Hell for sinners, belief in an eternal paradise, belief in a physical or spiritual resurrection, and so on. We would then get results that demonstrated that, out of a sampling of 10,000 members of a given denomination, such and such a percentage believe in hellfire, another view Hell as separation from God, and other percentages hold variations of these views.

The real issues surrounding death and dying surface when one is actually facing death—one's own or the death of a loved one. It is then that one struggles with feelings of loss, separation, guilt, frustration, and anger. And, when that death is accompanied by intractable pain or on-going coma, issues of ethical response to the situation, legal and theological prescriptions, and feelings of love and caring compete. In such circumstances, answers provided in response to a general survey may be ignored.

1

Because survey instruments must, by their very nature, impose upon the time of the respondents, they need to be brief and succinct. At the same time, they must leave no question in the mind of the respondent concerning the nature of the issue involved. For instance, we assumed that not everyone would know the difference between "active" and "passive" euthanasia. It was necessary to spell out details.

On the other hand, significant details had to be omitted lest the questionnaire exceed two pages, the generally accepted maximum length. For example, it had to be assumed that the reader would know that all reasonable treatments for the diseases mentioned in the questionnaire had been exhausted and that the patient's condition was irreversible; also, it was assumed that in- or outpatient care, the potential discomforts of continuing care, and the financial resources of the patient and family had been explored. If all of these factors had been considered and if the patient would continue in intractable pain and be kept alive in a hospital setting at great expense and discomfort, would the judgment concerning euthanasia be affected? None of these special circumstances could be sufficiently explored in the questionnaire, but certainly the context of each case is important.

Nor was there opportunity to inquire into the personal involvement of the clergy with cases of terminal illness. In phone conversations, some clergy made it clear that their responses were colored by awareness of difficulties surrounding terminal illness in parishioners or in members of their own families. It is a simple matter to quote the regulations provided by a religious organization as guidelines; it is quite a different matter to be confronted on a personal level with imminent death and suffering.

For these and other reasons, the survey must be seen as a beginning. The discomfort I have found among fellow therapists when they are confronted with situations involving euthanasia is not too different from that experienced by health practitioners and the clergy. Guidelines concerning passive euthanasia have been developed by some groups. Medical personnel are always helped when clear statements of support and guidance come from ethicists, theologians, and the clergy. But, even with such guidance, the practice of medicine remains under severe scrutiny.

In general, suicide has been judged a crime against God and considered a sin because, according to some theology, the deity gave life and only the deity should determine when life ends. Yet, interestingly enough, suicide appears to have been accepted in the religions of many ancient societies. For example, suicide is not specifically condemned or prohibited in the Bible, unless the commandment "Thou shalt not kill" (which is correctly translated "You shall not commit homicide") be interpreted to include suicide. King Saul and his armor-bearer committed suicide rather than fall into the hands of the enemy Philistines (I Sam. 31:4–5; I Chron. 10:4–5). There was no condemnation. Nor was King Zimri of Israel faulted when he died in a fire he himself had ignited at a time of desperation (I Kings 16:15–20). When Ahitophel, King David's counselor, hanged himself there was no denouncement of him and he was buried in his family tomb (II Sam. 17:23). Nor was Judas condemned when he hanged himself (Matt. 27:5).

Despite the lack of condemnation of suicide in the Bible, the early Christian church did move away from it as an acceptable way to end life. St. Augustine (A.D. 354–430) condemned suicide as a violation of the VI commandment. Later, St. Thomas Aquinas (1225–1274) argued that the act was a mortal sin: he declared that it was contrary to natural law, damaging to the human community, and symbolic of humans usurping divine prerogatives concerning decisions of life and death. Such attitudes have become the heritage of the Christian Church and particularly the Roman Catholic Church—and hence of society in general.

Traditionally, Roman Catholic clergy have refused funeral rites and burial in consecrated grounds to suicide victims. Church cemeteries had separated areas of interment for anyone who had died without the blessings of the church. Fenced off from sacred grounds (and often untended and overgrown with weeds), these graves became stark reminders of the church's rejection of anyone who violated religious taboos.

In recent years, however, there has been a change. Many Catholic priests do not refuse church rites nor burial in Roman Catholic cemeteries to victims of suicide. These priests acknowledge that social forces and the complex pressures of modern existence often confuse and disorient individuals. It becomes impossible to fix responsibility and blame solely upon the victim; society is also accountable.

Protestant and Jewish clergy also tend to treat the issue of suicide with compassion and understanding. For those who belong to Ethical Culture and Humanist groups, suicide is viewed as one way of terminating life and there is no condemnation of the individual. No guilt is fixed on the friends and family of the deceased person. On the other hand, suicide is prohibited among Muslims as a violation of the divine will and the teachings of the Quran. Those who take their own lives are excluded from the Muslim paradise.

Religions, of course, operate on two levels: a rational, intellectual level, and an affect level. On the intellectual level, the wrestling with issues and ideals leads, it is hoped, to position statements based on logic and fact. For the masses, the affect level is often colored by teachings concerning rewards for obedience and punishments for deviance. The conditioning dictum appears to be "hear and obey."

On the other hand, simply because a religious organization makes a pronouncement, there is no guarantee that the masses will follow. Practical considerations often intervene. Perhaps the notable example comes from Italy: when the Pope attacked the use of birth control as not in keeping with teachings of the Church and the Church's interpretation of divine will, Catholic women in Rome, living within the shadow of the Vatican, refused to conform. They continue to attend Mass and call themselves Catholic, but they also continue to enjoy sexual intercourse and keep their families small. They ignore the decree.

So, too, regarding euthanasia: when a parishioner or follower of a given religion is faced with unremitting pain and a terminal disease, he or she (or a loved one) may choose to ignore the teachings of religion and state and become involved in suicide, assisted suicide, or even murder (which Derek Humphry has aptly named "the compassionate crimes"). This fact suggests that what is said in this study should be tempered with the reality of human behavior.

It should also be noted that the questionnaire limits the discussion of euthanasia to the terminally ill. It does not include the termination of life by those who may be painfully afflicted but are not terminally ill. Nor does it embrace the plight of the emotionally distraught, who find the pressures of life overwhelming and wish to commit suicide. By limiting the discussion to those suffering terminal illness, the concerns about potential excesses as expressed in so-called "wedge" or "domino" theories or "slippery-slope" arguments are avoided. James M. Childs, Jr., writing in *Currents in Theology and Mission*, commented:

> This "wedge" or "domino" theory envisions a parade of horrors that recalls the Nazi experience. An irresponsible use of direct euthanasia could also lead to a calloused disregard for human life. A Florida physician/legislator, Dr. W. Sackett, for example, suggested that the state could save five billion dollars over the next fifty years if all the mongoloids were allowed to succumb to the pneumonia they frequently contract.

The questionnaire has attempted to show that nothing would be done without awareness of the expressed wishes of the patient. Such desires would have been included in a Living Will and would have been filed with an attorney, medical personnel, the family, and the clergy, if appropriate. Although such issues were not raised in direct response to the questionnaire, views on Living Wills appear in materials returned by respondents and in articles in religious journals.

Most persons do not die agonizing deaths marked by prolonged suffering. Much terminal pain can be controlled by medication, and there are many physicians who do not use extreme or heroic measures to prolong life. On the other hand, there are cases where the nature of the terminal illness necessitates delicate moral and ethical decisions on the part of the dying person and his or her loved ones. In one instance, intractable pain and the use of palliatives may reduce the patient to a semi-comatose state, unable to think or to communicate coherently; he or she becomes virtually numb to all that goes on in their environment. In another case, a patient may move into a coma where cognitive powers are seriously damaged and the patient sinks into a "vegetative" state, kept alive by the miracles of modern chemistry and bio-engineering.

It is in such circumstances that the question arises: What is the proper thing to do—terminate life and shorten the time of suffering, or use every medical means available to prolong life? Does one disconnect the life-support system and let the patient die, or does one continue to employ what have been called "heroic" measures to sustain life? (The term "heroic" refers to treatment that will not benefit the patient by relieving pain or curing the disease: it simply prolongs living, regardless of the lack of quality of the patient's life.)

Of course, the best known recent confrontation of faith and heroic measures came in the Karen Ann Quinlan case. The Quinlans' family priest, the Rev. Thomas Trapasso, is reported to have said, "I believe a person doesn't have a constitutional right to die. . . . But I believe a person has a constitutional right to decide how to die in the framework of life-sustaining machines." The vice-chancellor of Father Trapasso's diocese, the Rev. Herbert Tillyer, added, "Once a judgment is reached by doctors that a person's situation is truly terminal and without hope, then there is no moral obligation to continue heroic or extraordinary measures or to continue life" (reported by Russell Chandler in "The Question," *Los Angeles Times,* Nov. 4, 1975).

In this case, the family had the support of the Church and complied with its teachings. But Karen Ann Quinlan continues to live after the "heroic" measures stopped. Today (end of 1984) she remains in an irreversible coma, oblivious, as far as anyone can tell, to anything in the external world. Her parents continue to visit, but there is no communication. To go beyond the withdrawal of life-support systems would be to become involved in "active" euthanasia. This the Quinlans, their physicians, and their clergy will not sanction.

The confusion of feelings that may be engendered when well-meaning, devout Christians accede to a patient's request for "no heroic measures" was made clear in a letter published in *Christianity Today,* Feb. 5, 1982, pp. 28–9. Grace P. Chapman, who, with her husband, has served as a missionary with the Evangelical Alliance Mission, wrote about the terminal illness of her father who, "because of a fast-growing cancer on his face, heart trouble, a diabetic condition, an operation for cancer of the colon five years ago, and a urinary blockage . . . requested his family not to take extraordinary measures to keep him alive should he seem to be near death." When he had a stroke that left him paralyzed and unable to swallow, Mrs. Chapman, the family, and the doctor agreed to keep the man as comfortable as possible, providing intravenous fluids but no other source of nourishment. Five weeks later, her father was still alive—aware, but unable to communicate. The life forces within him were stronger than anticipated. Mrs. Chapman wrote: "What we have done is predetermine that, if Dad does not die soon of a heart attack or cancer or some other sudden infirmity, he will die of starvation." She wrote of her feelings of guilt. She questioned whether anyone had the right to make choices concerning one's own death or the death of another. She asked, "Where does trusting God begin and where does it end in this particular situation?"

She states, "If God had 'cooperated' in the beginning, we would have said with deep feeling, as Job did, 'The Lord gave, the Lord has taken away. Blessed be the name of the Lord.' Since God has not seen fit to take him yet, it is harder to say 'Blessed be the name of the Lord.' Will Dad's final act of dying be one that God has ordained at that time, or will it be the result of our maneuvering?" She wonders: "If there are no situations in life that, no matter which direction we take, we lack a perfect peace, a perfect assurance that 'this is the way, walk in it.'"

In the same issue of *Christianity Today*, Dr. Jeanne Blumhagen, a former medical missionary and a practicing physician, wrote a response to Mrs. Chapman entitled "We Cannot Choose in a Moral Vacuum" (pp. 29–30):

> We will and do make mistakes. Heroic measures will bring one back to vigorous life, while another will have permanent brain damage or prolonged suffering. We must learn to live with this inequality. We may find that our knowledge was limited, our predictions wrong, and that the Lord has other plans. This, too, we must accept as from his hand. . . .
>
> Ultimately, the choice lies with him. When we have done what we could in a loving, responsible way, it is no longer ours to determine. It rests in the sovereignty of God. The stress will remain, along with the perplexities that force us to run to the Lord and learn to rest in him.

Mr. Joseph Bayly, vice-president of David C. Cook Publishing Company, also responded in his article, "Is it Life or Death that is Prolonged?" (pp. 30–31). He wrote:

I agree with your statement about not necessarily having perfect peace when you do what you perceive to be the will of God. So many of life's decisions are not between right and wrong, but between alternative choices, both of which may be right or (more often) wrong. To admit our fallibility, our dependence on God, and then to make what seems to be the better (or less worse) choice is all that we can do.

And in making such a choice we trust in the sovereign God, who can undo our choices, changing consequences if we are wrong, and forgive our sin of ignorance. Often, as you indicate, there is no peace— only assurance that God is in control, whatever we may do, and knows our intentions were good and designed to do his will.

The last response was from Dr. Gordon L. Addington, formerly a medical missionary and now a practicing surgeon. In his reply "There May Be No Absolute Answer," Dr. Addington assured Mrs. Chapman:

. . . that God is lovingly involved and sovereign in the lives of each of his children—in this instance, both the patient and the family members attempting to make good decisions on behalf of their father.

While the judgment of individuals may vary with respect to what is appropriate, I believe that when God's children ask for guidance, they can trust him to give that guidance. We can also trust him to lead us to change an initial decision that might not be best. This conviction about God's active care for his children is a great comfort to me. As Christians, we ask for guidance, and do our best with information available in the light of the principles of Scripture. Then we can trust God.

Medicine, Religion, and Euthanasia

Obviously the patient and the family cannot make decisions to remove life-support equipment or to withhold treatment without the consent and participation of the physician. And the medical profession has been wrestling with their responsibilities to patients and their families. On December 4, 1973, the House of Delegates of the American Medical Association adopted the following statement:

> The intentional termination of life of one human being by another— mercy killing—is contrary to that for which the medical profession stands and is contrary to the policy of the American Medical Association.
>
> The cessation of the employment of extraordinary means to prolong the life of the body when there is irrefutable evidence that biological death is imminent is the decision of the patient and/or his immediate family. The advice and judgment of the physician should be freely available to the patient and/or his immediate family.

The validity of this stance has been challenged by James Rachels, who suggests that there may well be occasions when active euthanasia is more humane than passive, where decisions concerning life and death on the basis of this pronouncement may be made on irrelevant grounds, and that the distinction between killing and letting someone die has no moral importance ("Active/Passive Euthanasia," *The New England Journal of Medicine,* Jan. 9, 1975).

One can only begin to estimate the degree of confusion that must exist among medical practitioners and their clients concerning the ethical, religious, moral, and theological dimensions of euthanasia. Some religious organizations adopt a firm stand. Others have not discussed the subject, while still others have left the matter open, preferring to let anyone involved with an end-of-life illness make his or her own decision. Medical doctors and nurses have wrestled with these issues for years. From articles in medical journals, the confusion and pain associated with such decisions can be clearly ascertained.

What are the issues and what can the clergy do to help?

There is the need to know that the ailing individual is actually dying, is in intractable pain, or is in a truly irreversible coma. There are practitioners who contend that "no one really knows when death is inevitable" (Frank J. Ayd, Jr. "The Hopeless Case," *The Journal of the American Medical Association,* Vol. 181, No. 13,

Sept. 1962, p. 1099). Numerous cases of the rescuing of apparently hopeless cases can be cited. For example, Gary Stocks was mugged and severely beaten about the head; for six weeks he remained paralyzed and in a coma. His doctors predicted that he would never be other than "a vegetable." However, the young man recovered, and at the age of 26 resumed his doctoral studies. Doctors called his recovery "unbelievable" (reported in the *Los Angeles Times,* Jan. 7, 1973).

Similarly, Carol Dusold was 19 years old when she was involved in an accident that broke her left arm and severely bruised her brain stem. In the ensuing months she was in a coma, and wasted away to 65 pounds—with her body twisted into a grotesque position. A doctor told her mother that all they could do "is try to starve her by taking the intravenous out." The mother, a devout Lutheran, refused and for four months maintained a vigil at her daughter's bedside, talking to the comatose girl, touching her, administering love. Carol recovered, married, bore a child and presently suffers only from a slight limp, a mild speech impediment, and a left hand permanently curled (reported in the *Los Angeles Times,* Dec. 3, 1975).

Medicine, Law, and the Living Will

Such cases raise issues concerning the Living Will and the exactness with which competent, caring physicians can predict the future of a patient or determine for sure when one has permanently entered the "vegetative state." On the other hand, there is the case of Karen Ann Quinlan, who has been comatose since April, 1975 and today (in 1984) is a 70-pound non-communicating, non-aware person coiled in a fetal position. When the respiratory system was removed in May, 1976, she continued to breath, and she did not die. Throughout the entire ordeal, the Quinlans have had the support of the Roman Catholic Church, for legal advice as well as spiritual comfort. (Earlier, in December, 1975, the New Jersey Catholic Conference, representing the state's four Catholic bishops, had filed a brief with the Supreme Court sup-

porting the father's request to become a guardian for the unconscious girl so the artificial support systems could be removed. The
medical practitioners were hesitant and delayed complying with the
Quinlan request until compelled to cooperate. These medical doctors were burdened with the questions of right and wrong, with
medical ethics, and with the problem of who should make the
decision. The last question was answered: the court made the
decision.)

Legal judgments can vary from place to place, however. In December, 1975, Duval County Circuit Judge John S. Cox in Jack-
sonville, Florida, ordered that Mrs. Celia Cain's respirator be
disconnected for 45 minutes so that Mrs. Cain might be permitted
to die as her husband had requested. If the woman had continued
to show signs of life after that time, the machine would have been
reconnected (as reported in the *Los Angeles Times*, Dec. 5, 1976).
There were no such signs. Mrs. Cain died.

On the other hand, just one month earlier, Circuit Court Judge
William Corrigan in St. Louis County, Missouri, ruled that doctors
could not shut off the life-support systems as requested by Gary
Debro, whose wife Judith Ann Debro had been in a coma for three
months as a result of an automobile accident (reported in the *Los
Angeles Times*, Nov. 28, 1975). Such diversity of opinion indicates
the need for further clarification of legal responsibilities and guidance for passive euthanasia for the medical profession.

Psychosocial Aspects

What is also clear is that many medical practitioners
are not prepared to deal with some of the psychosocial dimensions
of dying and death. Their training has prepared them as rescuers
from illness and pain, and physicians may see themselves as arch-
rivals of death. However, through the developments of medical
engineering and pharmaceuticals, terminal illness, pain, and dying
have assumed different dimensions. Formerly lethal illnesses can
now be controlled. Pain that once seemed to be intractable can be
kept in check by palliatives. Mechanized devices take charge of

breathing and heart beat, kidney functions, and other physical faculties.

At the same time, medical personnel confront new dimensions of the healing arts: the ethics involved in keeping persons alive permanently damaged by severe brain injury and with no hope of recovery, the ethics of refusing lethal medication that would terminate suffering in terminal illnesses, and the coping patterns developed by those dealing with their own death—or with the losses associated with the death of a loved other. Many doctors feel alone and without adequate guidelines and with no place to turn for help. Some simply accept the teachings provided by a given religious group, and, insofar as the doctors work in institutions controlled by that group and treat patients associated with that particular religion, follow the guidelines provided. Others are torn. Some act on their own best judgment.

The call for bioethical courses appearing in medical journals is not surprising. During the years 1971–72, Vanderbilt University School of Medicine offered an elective course for 14 third-and-fourth year medical students entitled, "Psychosocial Aspects of Life-Threatening Illness" (reported in *The Journal of Medical Education*, Vol. 47, December 1972, pp. 945–51, by Berton, Flexner, van Eys, and Scott). The course involved readings from the classics, role-playing, interviews with terminally ill persons, clergy, pastoral counselors, and with medical personnel who dealt with the terminally ill. Similar courses have been given elsewhere with varying degrees of success. Much depends upon the leadership. A great deal depends upon the skill of psychotherapists to elicit responses, and many counselors—not unlike their medical counterparts—are uncomfortable with the subject of dying. They have yet to work through their own feelings on life and death.

Most medical personnel and psychotherapists have little or no familiarity with the ways in which the different religions of the world confront death, nor with their responses to issues involved in euthanasia. When Karen Ann Quinlan was on a respirator, the clergy of the Roman Catholic Church were more receptive to the abandonment of heroic measures of treatment than were the medical staff, perhaps because they deal more directly with the pain involved with loss and grief. Still, in preparing them to be rabbis, priests, or ministers, most pastoral training focuses on rites of passage, the role of the clergy and theological doctrines related to death, rather than on the very real processes of grief, loss, emptiness, and the fears of the dying person and the stricken family. Certainly few members of the clergy are alerted to ways in which different members of the family, including very young children, respond to death and bereavement, and of the scars that can remain.

Because the use of heroic treatment has troubled physicians for centuries, certain general moral and ethical guidelines have been developed. Doctors cannot "ethically or legally apply any remedy without the patient's knowledge and consent. The mere fact that a person presents himself for treatment indicates implicit consent for the ordinary therapeutic measures employed by the medical profession, but it does not authorize the application of extraordinary methods of treatment" (Frank J. Ayd, Jr., M.D., "The Hopeless Case," *The Journal of the American Medical Association*, Vol. 181, No. 13, Sept. 29, 1962, p. 1101). In cases where the patient is not able to give consent, permission must be sought from those empowered to give consent—and that consent must be freely given. It is only when the patient is unable to grant consent that the physician, using his or her best wisdom, may have to determine the best course of action. But even here, full consideration of patient rights—the expected results of treatment, the risks involved, and the purpose of the extreme measure—must be accounted for.

The Crucial Situation

Just how is a decision to be made in a crucial situation? Does a panel of experts pronounce the correct moral stance, the ethical-legal issues, the religious factors, the psychological and social implications of treatment versus non-treatment? In a discussion concerned with the use of ethical "experts" called to testify on ethical issues in a court of law, Richard Delago indicates that these experts should include philosophers, ethicists, theologians, and clergy ("Moral Experts in the Court? The Jury is Still Out," *The Center Magazine*, March/April 1984, pp. 48–64).

Some doctors risk taking matters into their own hands. In an interview in Washington D.C. in 1975, Dr. Christiaan Barnard, of South Africa, stated that he had let patients die "to prevent suffering" for the patient and for those who care (*Los Angeles Times*, October 27, 1975). In November 1974, Dr. George Maier, of Scotland, published an autobiography entitled *Confessions of a Surgeon* in which he admits to providing a patient with an enormous dosage of lethal drugs at her request. In a press interview, he suggested that he and other doctors often administer lethal drugs to terminally ill patients (Harry Trimborn, "Small Talk, Tea . . . and Death; Mercy Killing 'Widespread,'" *Los Angeles Times*, November 8, 1974). Dr. Alby Hartman of Cape Town, South Africa, admitted administering a lethal dosage of sodium pentathol to terminate the suffering of his 87-year-old cancer-stricken father. He was sentenced to one-year suspended sentence (*Los Angeles Times*, March 21 and 22, 1975)

On the other, Alfred Jaretzki, Associate Clinical Professor of Surgery, College of Physicians, Columbia University, and member of the Medical Advisory Committee of the Euthanasia Educational Council, stated that "physicians should disassociate themselves from any activities related to the promotion of active euthanasia." He added: "Should active euthanasia ever become a reality, physicians must have no more than a consulting role in the selection of individuals for its enactment and must take absolutely no part in its implementation" ("Death with Dignity—Passive Euthanasia," *The New York State Journal of Medicine*, April 1976, pp. 539–543).

His definition of active euthanasia reduces the act to simple killing. He writes that it "refers to the deliberate act of taking a human being's life, albeit with the intention of benefiting the individual and/or society as a whole. When one actively intercedes to produce death, regardless of the motive, whether with mercy or malevolence, it is killing." This definition conveniently removes active euthanasia from the medical scene. Equally important, it ignores the plight of a terminally ill patient in intractable pain who requests help in dying from the physician or from anyone who cares about the patient's feelings.

Jaretzki does, however, support physician involvement in *passive* euthanasia, which he defines as allowing "a patient who is dying, whose time has come, to die in a dignified manner as comfortably as possible." He limits his definition of passive euthanasia to refer "specifically and exclusively to a physician and his patient and not to two individuals in any other relationship . . . to the physician's acts of allowing a patient to die whose time has come, who is dying, where death is inevitable, but not to letting an individual die in any other context . . . to withholding treatment that would prolong the dying process . . . to permitting nature to take its course and not directly causing life to end by an overt act . . . and to allowing this death to occur with as much dignity as possible, avoiding useless, in these instances, degrading, and heroic procedures that do prolong the misery of dying and in themselves cause additional pain and discomfort."

Further, he emphasizes an open discussion about death, the importance of the Living Will, and recommends that the hospital room be open to visits by friends and family of all ages, arguing that "the physician not only has the moral and legal authority to allow his terminal patient to die in dignity but, in my opinion, has the clear obligation to do so as well." His guidelines for the physician include questions as to whether or not all "reasonable" treatments have been employed, whether further treatment will merely prolong "misery and hospitalization before death occurs anyway," the degree of discomfort and risk involved in continuing treatment, the nature of any further treatment (established or experimental), and the financial resources of the patient and family.

The formula is cautious and is one that finds support in statements by many religious groups. What is of importance is that in Jaretzki 's statements on passive euthanasia, the patient, not the doctor, is placed at the center. The patient's feelings, needs, and well-being are central, rather than the doctor's commitment to healing at all costs. The patient is given the opportunity to decide about treatment after having been given the best information available. His or her comfort and the feelings of the family are uppermost, not the battle against the disease, which has already been lost.

One of the most common objections to euthanasia is the argument that a miraculous cure may be just around the corner. This hope is, of course, not beyond the range of possibility. The case most often cited is that of George R. Minot, who, between 1921 and 1923, was losing the battle against diabetes. Then insulin was discovered and he lived to win a Nobel Prize for research that brought about a cure for pernicious anemia. Such cases are rare— but they do exist.

Another objection lies in the hope that the physician may have misdiagnosed the ailment; this too is not beyond the range of possibility. But diagnostic errors can be checked by getting several medical opinions. Although there is still a possibility of error, the "other opinion" approach is a reasonable safeguard.

The most common objection found among certain religious groups is that because God gave life, only God should take it away. Any intervention in the natural process signifies humans "playing God." Robert Wennberg suggests that this interpretation could prevent intervention "to save a man's life in circumstances when otherwise he would die a natural death" ("Euthanasia; A Sympathetic Appraisal," *Christian Scholars Review,* April 7, 1977, pp. 281–302). Even the insertion of pace-setters to control heart beat could be viewed as "an usurption of God's sovereignty over life as it works itself out in the natural order. But, of course, this we don't believe."

Wennberg writes that the Bible indicates that nature as well as man is "fallen," and refers to Genesis 3:16–19, where it is stated that the ground is cursed because of the disobedience of Adam and Eve, and to Romans 8:18–23, in which the Apostle Paul, writing to the Christian community in Rome, reflects the Genesis concept. Paul writes of "the creation" having been "subjected to futility," "groaning in travail" and anticipating freedom in salvation. On this basis, Wennberg suggests that "the natural order does not

perfectly express God's will, just as we human beings do not perfectly express his will either." He continues:

> Accordingly we wrestle with nature to channel it in directions we
> discern to be expressive of God's will . . . Therefore, we need not au-
> tomatically assume that a natural but lengthy and terribly painful death
> is to be accepted simply because it is natural. On the contrary, why
> should we not seek to control the dying process (in this case shortening
> it) in ways we discern to be expressive of kindness and compassion,
> and consequently in keeping with God's will, not because natural, but
> because rendered responsive to mercy and love?

He suggests that the "leave it to nature" argument stems from
a desire, perhaps an unconscious one, "to avoid responsibility for
what is happening when a patient is suffering." We reason: "It is
God's responsibility, not ours . . ." Thus we can, in good conscience,
step back and leave it to God.

Wennberg argues, "We must assume our responsibility" when
it is "in our power to shorten an agonizing death by intervening
and we do not do so." Then he states: "We are responsible for the
consequences of not doing." He quotes the Roman Catholic theologian Charles Curran, who wrote in *Politics, Medicine, and Christian Ethics* (Philadelphia: Fortress Press, 1973, pp. 161–162):
"Precisely because the dying process has now begun, man's positive
intervention is not an arrogant usurping of the role of God, but
rather in keeping with the process which is now encompassing the
person."

Wennberg points out that suffering in terminal illness is pointless
and is not to be endured as part of the cure. Nor should the suffering
be borne to discharge social and family responsibilities, for the
terminal patient is not in any position to discharge such responsibilities. He quotes the Rev. John McElhenney, who wrote in *Cutting
the Monkey-Rope* (Valley Forge, Pennsylvania, Judson Press, 1973,
p. 110):

> Such grasping for straws is not necessary for the Christian. He believes
> that his dying has been caught up in the death and resurrection of Jesus
> Christ. As birth is a gift of God, so is death. Therefore, the Christian

is not bound to strive officiously to prolong that living which is truly dying. Christ harrowed hell. Death does not cut the man-God monkey-rope. Hence, it is not obligatory to fetch hell into the hospital room by prolonging the agony of dying. The doctor may permit death to enter as a conquered enemy who is now to be greeted as a friend.

It is clear that much discussion lies ahead before any general consensus will be found. Cognitive approaches are important in helping to clarify definitions, patterns, and potential consequences. But when the actual confrontation with painful terminal illness is involved, quite often the reasoned theological and ethical responses become secondary. One responds, not irrationally, to the affect—not irrationally—because new immediate feeling premises have become paramount. Some examples of the struggle/conflict can be seen in the responses from the various religious groups presented in the following sections.

Judaism

Although neither the World Jewish Congress (an umbrella organization for Jewish groups of varying viewpoints) nor the Union of American Hebrew Congregations has taken any official stand on the issue of euthanasia, the subject has been discussed in Jewish journals.

With regard to active euthanasia, the Jewish position seems clear. Immanuel Jacobovitz, whose work is often cited (*Jewish Medical Ethics*, N.Y. Bloch, 1959, pp. 123–4) stated:

> It is clear, then, that, even when the patient is already known to be on his deathbed and close to the end, any form of *active euthanasia* is strictly prohibited. In fact, it is condemned as plain murder. In purely legal terms, this is borne out by the ruling that anyone who kills a dying person is liable to the death penalty as a common murderer. At the same time, Jewish law sanctions, and perhaps even demands, the withdrawal of any factor—whether extraneous to the patient himself or not—which may artificially delay his demise in the final phase. It might be argued that this modification implies the legality of expediting the death of an incurable patient in acute agony by withholding from him such medicaments as sustain his continued life by unnatural means. . . . Our sources advert only to cases in which death is expected to be imminent; it is, therefore, not altogether clear whether they would tolerate this moderate form of euthanasia, though that cannot be ruled out.

19

The Karen Ann Quinlan case and the passing of the California Natural Death Act, in 1976, triggered a series of Jewish essays. For example, the journal *Sh'ma,* in the April 15, 1977 edition, published a number of responses by Jewish writers to the Death Act and to the provisions for a Living Will. Elliot Horowitz wrote:

> The Natural Death Act primarily gives an individual a degree of authority in choosing his style of death when the Rider of the Pale Horse beckons: whether to "go gentle into that good night" or "to rage against the dying of the light." But whether the State now sanctions the trespass by man into the realm of the divine or whether it has merely allowed him to reclaim a right usurped by modern technology—the right to opt for death unfettered by man-made machines—is ultimately at the heart of the issue.

The freedom to be in control of one's demise was of importance to several writers, particularly those of liberal persuasion. Hillel Cohn commented that "The liberal Jew who does not consider himself bound by *halacha*—he may choose that course of action which is most humanizing and will in no way diminish the prospects of a more just society." He insisted that "the right to die" was a fundamental freedom to be used with "the utmost of responsibility":

> It is a Jewish religious act to choose natural death. The Natural Death Act enables the Jew, I feel, to perform a religious act of the highest quality. It enables the Jew to consider his or her life and death and to make some responsible determination as to what he or she wishes done, in the event that he or she is suffering from an incurable injury or illness.

Not all contributors agreed. J. David Bleich argued:

> In point of fact, the California statute does not at all strike a blow for human freedom; it serves but to legislate recognition of disparity in the value of human life. The legislature is saying that some life is more sacred than others. The remaining life span of the terminal patient is not of much value, therefore it may be foreshortened with impunity. This is a value judgment which can—and should—be disputed. But to identify this dubious judgment as a realization of human freedom is a sham and should be recognized as such.

Seymour Siegel dealt with the question of whether the Living Will might not be considered a sanctioning of suicide:

> The question may be asked whether the Living Will is not a form of suicide. From the point of view of common sense, suicide is the willful taking of one's own life. Jewish law is very insistent on the presence of *willfulness,* which is defined as a philosophical disgust with life. This is a denial of providence. . . . By allowing death to come when it is imminent, a person is hardly denying providence. He is permitting God's judgment to take its effect, without the intervention of useless, artificial means.
>
> A Jewish living will is in keeping with tradition. One could ask: "Isn't every moment of life precious whether sustained by artificial means or not?" Judaism is a religion of life. However, the mere functioning of physical systems is not the ultimate good.

Moshe D. Tendler included references to the phrase "death with dignity," which he labelled "an ill-conceived slogan":

> Death with dignity is the end result of a dignified life style. In itself, death is a truly undignified behavior. If those attending the dying patient behave in sensitive, dignified fashion, no indignity other than that of death itself is involved.
>
> A treatment modality that prolongs or accentuates pain without hope of cure is indeed to be questioned on ethical, moral grounds. If the patient chooses to continue treatment, despite the discomfort it causes or prolongs, he is entitled to the full support of the health profession. If he requests the discontinuance of therapy, emphasizing his inability to cope with his pain-filled existence, the absence of any real hope for cure makes this request binding on all who minister to him.

He concludes with a statement concerning ethical aesthetics:

> If continuation of life support systems after the point of no return will emphasize our commitment to the infinite worth of man and prevent the callus that forms on the soul when a "plug is pulled," it is money well spent. God forbid that we ever reach the time when the true triage must be practiced, with "God committees" deciding who gets the respirator or kidney dialysis equipment and lives, and who dies.

These quotations indicate that there is a definite rejection of active euthanasia in Jewish religious thought; the dialogue on passive euthanasia is still open. Underlying each position are the Jewish scriptures, particularly the Torah or Law, the Talmudic *halakah* or interpretations of oral traditions—the so-called "unwritten law"—and modern Jewish learning. For example, Teodoro Forcht Dagi, writing in *Judaism,* in the Spring issue of 1975, notes that the Talmud refers to Proverbs 31:6, "Give strong drink to one about to perish . . . ", and to the discussion in Hillel relating this verse to a criminal about to be executed. He writes, "The range of acts which halakhah permitted, and even required, indicates that the deontological codification had a strong sense of mercy and a deep sensitivity to suffering." In this passage from Proverbs and its interpretation he finds "a precedent . . . for relieving the suffering of one about to die." He continues:

> Medically speaking, the Talmud recognised a state of moribundity called *gosses*. A patient was called *gosses* when he could no longer swallow his saliva (*Even Haezer,* cxxi, 7). It is generally assumed that this state would last no more than three days (*Yoreh Deah,* cccxxxix. 2). According to some authorities, even if a patient cannot swallow his saliva, if he can be kept alive for more than three days, he is not *gosses* (Rabbi David Bleich, New York, personal communication). Even in this state, however, the patient must be considered a living being, and does not give up any of his rights as a living Jew. Whoever removes the pillow from under the head of a patient who is *gosses,* or does anything at all which hastens his death, is considered criminally culpable of having shed blood (*Yoreh Deah,* cccxxxix. 1). Jakobovits discusses Isserles' amplification of the point forbidding the removal of a pillow from under the head of a *gosses.* (Jakobovits: *Jewish Medical Ethics,* pp. 122–3)

>> It is forbidden to cause the dying to pass away quickly; for instance, if a person is in a dying condition for a long time and he cannot depart, it is prohibited to remove the pillow or the cushion from underneath him following the popular belief that feathers from some birds have this effect.

Other sources also concur that the life of a dying person must be seen as so delicate that it is threatened by even the smallest movement. Any threat to the thread of life is clearly prohibited. There is some qualification, however; according to the *Sefer Hasidim,* one is prohibited from committing an action which would extend the dying process (*Sefer Hasidim,* nos. 234 and 723).

Active euthanasia is thus prohibited, and one who kills a dying person is subject to the laws dealing with simple murderers (cf. *Sanhedrin* 78a, and Jakobovits, *Op. cit.* p. 306, notes 44–47). Jakobovits indicates the possibility that passive euthanasia, as we have described it, might be acceptable where death is imminent, but his position is complicated by Bleich's restraint that if it is possible to keep a patient alive by some means for more than three days, even in the absence of the ability to swallow, he cannot be considered *gosses.* In short, while halakhah considers the matters of euthanasia and the dying patient at some length, it clearly prohibits active euthanasia, and gives no clear warrant permitting the withdrawal of life-supporting measures in the dying patient. The notion of brain death is altogether absent, although it must be noted that the condition of being unable to swallow one's saliva is equivalent to brainstem death in modern medical parlance, and destruction of the gag reflex. This degree of central nervous system death is not far removed from the definition of brain death now becoming more commonly accepted in medical circles. Consciousness *per se,* however, is not considered grounds for determination of the medical state. Death can be declared only when respiration ceases, and interference with the dying process previous to that is governed by the principles we have just mentioned.

Both by Jewish law and by secular law, the physician is advised to desist from active euthanasia. If it could be shown that a patient would die within three days in the absence of the initiation of a new therapy (the first component of passive euthanasia) *and* the patient were already *gosses,* a strong case might be made for therapeutic reticence. If the patient were not *gosses,* however, or if it were not certain that he would die within three days, even this warrant would be lacking. The discontinuation of a respirator is quite problematical, and appears to be absolutely prohibited under extant interpretations of halakhah. The consideration of passive euthanasia, then, at least according to halakhah, is perhaps different in principle from the consideration of active euthanasia, but not far removed in practice. Secular law seems more comfortable with some forms of passive euthanasia. The discontinuation of life support and the reluctance to initiate new therapy is not uncommonly discussed in daily medical practice. Both courses are essentially legitimatized in practice.

Other Jewish traditions have also been utilized. Simon Federbush, writing in *Judaism* (June, 1952), pointed out that Maimonides
(Hilkot Rotzeah II, 7) ruled that, "One who kills a healthy or a
dying person, or even a hopelessly sick man, is guilty of murder."
Federbush states that, "Not only is it forbidden to put an end to
the life of an incurable, but it is also obligatory to refrain from any
act which is bound to hasten the death of such a suffering person."
He applies these traditions to the death of those who do not give
their consent. To explicate a situation where one does give consent,
he refers to the biblical story of the death of King Saul (II Sam.
1:6–10). The young man who killed the king at the monarch's
request, when the dying ruler failed in his attempt to take his own
life, was put to death by King David. David said, "Your blood is
upon your head, for your words have testified against you, saying
I have killed the Lord's anointed one" (II Sam. 1:16). Federbush
concludes, "It is therefore obvious that already in ancient Israel it
was considered a crime to put to death a dying man, even at his
own request." Philip A. Bardfeld, writing in *Reconstructionist* (September 1976), notes that the death of the young man may have
been for political rather than ethical reasons. He notes also that
because the young man was an Amalakite and of a group that did
"not occupy a favored status in the Bible . . . it is unlikely that such
a person would be portrayed as performing a good deed or a socially
desirable act."

None of the writers referred to the other instance of so-called
"mercy killing" in the Bible. Abimelech is killed by his armor-bearer
after he had been fatally wounded by a millstone dropped by a
woman from the battlements during a siege. To avoid the ignominy
of being killed by a woman, Abimelech said to his armor-bearer,
"Draw your sword and kill me, lest men say of me, 'A woman
killed him'" (Judges 9:54). There is no condemnation of this killing
in the biblical text.

It is clear that the issue is not closed in Jewish circles. Bardfeld
reports that the Quinlan case provoked much discussion among
Jewish leaders. He notes that, in reference to this case, Rabbi Norman Lamm, the President of Yeshiva University, observed: "We are
not required to utilize heroic measures to prolong the life of hope-

lessly sick patients, but we are forbidden to terminate the use of such measures once they have begun. . . . If we are asked whether or not to use such extraordinary measures to prolong the life of a patient who has suffered irreversible brain damage, then there are grounds, depending on the individual case, for responding negatively, but Jewish law cannot sanction pulling the plug, which is tantamount to severing a vital organ of the patient, which is forbidden."

Bardman stated that Rabbi Seymour Siegel of the Jewish Theological Seminary gave his personal opinion that it was permissible to "remove the respirator in this case, and let nature take its course." Rabbi Joseph Perman of the Free Synagogue of Westchester said, "It would not be ethically justifiable to prolong the life of a person in a vegetative state for an indeterminate period of time," and that, "No parent, whether natural or adoptive, should ever have to beg that their child's life be taken."

Jewish ethics eschew any aspect of active euthanasia. The multiple dimensions of passive euthanasia are still *sub judice.*

Roman Catholicism

Perhaps no religious organization has been respon-
sible for more literature about euthanasia and the right to die than
the Roman Catholic Church. Publications in the various languages
of the world from countries where the Church is active abound.
They reflect the concerns of priests, theologians, philosophers, ethicists, and medical doctors who are confronted with the advance-
ments of modern medical achievements in prolonging life, even after
the quality of life has deteriorated—and even after the brain has
ceased to function on all but the most primitive levels. For example,
Roman Catholic ethicists (in Germany) are confronted with va-
garies in the concept of euthanasia, as they seek to distinguish
between 'help in dying' (*Sterbehilfe, Hilfe in Sterben*) and 'helping
to die' (*Sterbennachhilfe, Hilfe zum Sterben*).

In the United States, the Church has been confronted with at
least two highly publicized medical cases involving Roman Catholic
personnel in which the use of heroic measures to prolong life has
been challenged. One, the Karen Ann Quinlan case, cited earlier
(p. 6), and a second case, that of Brother Joseph Fox, an 83-year-
old Marianist Brother, who, in 1979, suffered cardiorespiratory
arrest after a routine hernia operation and the administration of
10 mg. of Valium. Heart massage restored the beat, but during the
arrest, due to an insufficient supply of oxygen to the brain, Brother
Fox suffered massive brain cell destruction which reduced him to

a chronic vegetative state. He was unable to speak, hear, move, think, or recognize anyone, and able to perform only the most primitive digestive processes. Because Pope Pius XII had noted, in a 1957 speech to anesthesiologists, that in keeping with Roman Catholic doctrine respirators could be considered "an extraordinary measure which need not be used to prolong life," the Marianist Brothers requested that Brother Fox's life be permitted to end naturally. The Nassau Hospital officials refused the request. The Nassau County District Attorney, pressured by right-to-life groups, warned that anyone who disconnected the apparatus would face prosecution for homicide. The Marianist Brothers petitioned the court for the removal of the life-support system.

When the case came to trial, because Brother Fox had previously made known his repugnance toward life in a vegetative state, the court granted the wishes of the Marianist community. The District Attorney appealed to the Appellate Court and that Court upheld the earlier decision. Again the attorney appealed—this time to the New York Court of Appeals, the highest court in the state. During the appeal, Brother Fox's heart gave out and he died. His case, the Quinlan case, and other similar examples were landmark cases of sorts: they confronted the Roman Catholic community, not with theoretical issues, but with real-life situations in which doctrine could be presented and still be rejected by local authorities.

Without question, the most important document pertaining to euthanasia is the Sacred Congregation for the Doctrine of the Faith's *Declaration on Euthanasia,* which was approved by Pope John Paul II and issued on May 5, 1980. It is published below in its entirety.

Prior to this publication, Pope John Paul II had made clear his stand on this issue. In an address to the Episcopal Conference of the United States on October 5, 1979, as reported in *The Pope Speaks,* Vol. 24:4, 1979, he commended the American clergy for their statement that "Euthanasia or mercy killing . . . is a grave moral evil . . . Such killing is incompatible with respect for human dignity and reverence for life." His position echoed that which had appeared earlier in *Gaudium et Spes,* the Pastoral Constitution of the Church in the Modern World, December 7, 1965, item 529, where euthanasia was grouped with murder, genocide, abortion, and wilful destruction, as among "whatever is opposed to life it-self." Pope Paul VI, in a message issued in union with the Synod of Bishops on October 23, 1974, in item 1210, stated:

> The right to life: This right is basic and inalienable. It is grievously violated in our day by abortion and euthanasia, by widespread torture, by acts of violence against innocent parties and by the scourge of war.*

It should be noted that right-to-life discussions have not been limited to scholarly works, but have spilled over into more popular Roman Catholic reading materials. Indeed, the document *Declaration on Euthanasia* has been published in booklet form, reprinted in numerous Roman Catholic publications, including the popular *Catholic Mind*. Beatriz K. Gomez, president of *Fundación Pro Derecho a Morir Dignamente* (Society for the Right to Die with Dignity) in Bogota, Colombia, notes that, "We feel that since Colombia has such strong ties with the Vatican, we strictly follow the Pope's ruling. DMD always includes with requests for '*Esta Es Mi Voluntad*,' Juan Pablo II's 'Declaration About Euthanasia' published here in Bogota in *El Tiempo*—June 27, 1980—a translation of the *New York Times* of the same date."

According to the Baroness Adrienne van Till (*Stichting Vrijwillige Euthanasia*) in the Netherlands, "The Roman Catholic Church, as represented by the Bishops, does not permit any active aid-in-dying, whether voluntary euthanasia or assisting suicide or mercy killing. They do permit so-called 'indirect euthanasia' . . . The Roman Catholic Church has circa 30% of the population." She adds: "Several Roman Catholic moralists (professors of ethics), however, admit in writing that in dramatic cases active voluntary euthanasia may be morally admissible as the lesser of two evils—if there is no other way to stop the patient's misery, and only if he asked for his death." What is most significant in this statement is that, despite the Vatican proclamation, the issues are still *sub judice*.

---

*The many articles associated with these pronouncements and with the *Declaration on Euthanasia* and the ethical, moral, and theological principles involved are far too complicated and numerous to consider here. Some are noted in the General Bibliography and with each article there are accompanying lists of further references.

One suspects that this is true elsewhere. For example, although the article was written before the publication of *Declaration on Euthanasia*, Dr. Russell L. McIntyre, director of Programs in the Health Care Humanities, College of Medicine and Dentistry, New Jersey, wrote in *Linacre Quarterly,* the official journal of the National Federation of Catholic Physicians' Guilds, an article titled "Euthanasia: A Soft Paradigm for Medical Ethics" (Vol. 45, Feb. 1978, pp. 41–54). In this essay, Dr. McIntyre states his intention "first, to encourage a new and healthy debate on all aspects of the euthanasia issue without loading the 'moral gun' before the debate begins; thus, I will purposefully not use the term 'killing' in my description because of its pejorative moral content; and second, to set forth a process understanding of life and death that might more adequately inform today's pastoral concerns." He reviews conservative and liberal positions, the familiar "wedge-domino-slippery slope" arguments, the pragmatic, relativist and subjective ethic arguments and then, "as an ethicist with a particular theological heritage," he presents "foundational assumptions of pastoral care," which include:

1. That we have an underlying sense of Christian values.
2. That we are dedicated persons in our professions—dedicated to the care of souls, as well as the care of bodies.
3. That we have a sense of ministry and mission in our work.
4. That we are competent in our work—that we are concerned about continuously examining our own lives, our own values, and how we do or do not communicate these values to others.
5. That we are essentially fulfilled persons: that we enjoy the challenges that life provides and are not always chafing at the bit.
6. That we are growth-oriented: that we have a thirst for knowledge, both in our medical or pastoral specialties, as well as in our quest for greater humanistic insights into life.

Having set forth these principles, McIntyre recognizes that euthanasia "may very well be a difficult testing ground for our sense of values." He insists:

that under no circumstances ought euthanasia be considered as an alternative to care. We have no moral ground on which to stand, whatever, if we euthanize to avoid care. The mandate of the medical profession is to provide care. All other values rank below this primary obligation. The mandates to promote life and relieve suffering can only be understood within the context of human care. To prolong life or to alleviate pain outside this context becomes an abuse of the medical privilege . . . What I am suggesting here is that the continuation of biological life is not the ultimate end value.

Having provided this basis for discussion, Dr. McIntyre turns to "specifics," all presented from a personal point of view in the light of the issues he has been discussing, and, of course, colored by his own theological commitments.

1. My conservative nature requires that I cling fast to the sanctity of life principle; that life is a sacred gift, given to us in trust by a loving God. But, I must also recognize that this gift, and the sacredness which accompanies it, also have limits; i.e., there comes a point in time when the gift is withdrawn and with that action the sacredness diminishes.

If we regard life as a gift from God, we must recognize that He gives it to us in trust that we will use it appropriately to our understanding of His love. In recognizing that life and its sacredness have limits, we are recognizing the trustfulness with which the gift of life is given. This, of course, has biblical precedence. In the Scriptures, both persons and places can have sacredness. And this special status can be lost, not only because of sin and defilement, but also because of the presence of God being withdrawn.

For me, this biblical distinction applies to life and death. The Spirit of God is given to create life; it is also withdrawn as life loses its vitality, its entelechy, as manifested in irreversible coma, a flat (or essentially flat) electroencephalogram, or being in a "persistent vegetative state." Charles Curran makes a distinction between the "process of living" and the "process of dying." The point at which the "process of dying" overtakes the "process of living" is when life-preserving therapies can be discontinued because they are inefficacious. For me, this is the withdrawal of that God-given sacredness which the gift possesses. My conservative nature requires me, therefore, to reject the need to prolong life as long as technically possible providing that certain base line criteria are established, e.g., the Harvard "brain death" or irreversible coma.

2. My more moderate nature forces me to recognize that under the rubric of care excruciating and intractable pain is also destructive to the sanctity of life. Here pain moves beyond the therapeutic bounds of "purifying the soul" and is diminutive to the sacredness of that life. Under the rubric of care our mandate is to relieve pain. If we can decrease pain, even with high dosages, without depressing any physical and conceptual powers, we must do it. But if we cannot, then our first obligation is to relieve pain.

Now, what I am suggesting might not be so different from what is, in fact, being done today in every hospital. With perhaps one exception. If this be passive euthanasia, let us recognize it as such and see it as one of our legitimate values of life within the rubric of care. We may wish to call it "terminal therapy" rather than euthanasia, but we must recognize that it is a different kind of therapy than chemo- or excisional therapy, which aim primarily at cure or remission. This is "terminal care therapy" and we should have no qualms about admitting it, to each other, to the family, and even to the patient, if this is still possible.

3. We must be very clear in our discussion of euthanasia as having a legitimate place in the medical mandate of care that we not be misunderstood. We must neither see euthanasia as an alternative to care nor suggest it for individuals who are not terminally ill, in intractable pain or irretrievably comatose. Here is the limit of my "soft" paradigm. We cannot morally extend it to persons not in a life-threatening terminal conditions. A distinction supplied by Paul Ramsey is important; a distinction between exceptions to a rule and exemptions from a rule.

The rule would be to provide life-sustaining therapies of care to all. The exception to this rule would be, as already described, persons terminally ill and irretrievably comatose or in intractable pain. Exemptions from even the consideration of euthanasia would be persons not in the terminal stages of dying, or to use the terms of Kamisar, the "congenital idiots . . . the permanently insane . . . the senile dementia." These may represent those in society who are not as pleasant to look at, or relate to, but they are not, and never ought to be, the candidates for social extermination.

It is important to note here that the present state of American case law makes this point explicitly clear. Normally law exists to protect innocent life, i.e., life that cannot protect itself. An example of this would be the ruling of Judge Muir at the Superior Court level in New Jersey that Karen Quinlan could not be removed from her life-sustaining respirator. However, the New Jersey State Supreme Court, in reversing

Judge Muir has provided an appropriate corrective to the belief that the law always protects life to the fullest extent, regardless of how terminally debilitated that life might actually be. The court ruled that:

> We think that the State's interest *contra* weakens and the individual's right to privacy grows as the degree of bodily invasion increases and the prognosis dims. Ultimately there comes a point at which the individual's rights overcome the State interest.

This is an extremely important legal step in morally recognizing that life has limits beyond which it ought not to be sustained. But the limits must be reached; and we cannot arbitrarily decide those limits. They are, as the court specified, to be determined medically, not socially.

If this guideline is followed, the "wedge argument" is countered. Human beings are capable of discriminating between cases and can appropriately decide when a life is beyond hope and beyond our ability to save. Yes, of course, there will be difficult cases, and cases which are not immediately clear. In these instances we must decide in favor of sustaining life. But, when the evidence is irrefutable, we must be able to express death as a positive value of life.

4. The only remaining question I wish to explore is the question of "who" should decide. Again the recent New Jersey Supreme Court Decision in the Case of Karen Quinlan is significant. Earlier, Judge Muir, in refusing to grant permission to remove her from the respirator, ruled that the decision was purely a medical decision. The family could make their request known, but the doctor must make the ultimate decision.

The Supreme Court ruling reversed Judge Muir and said that it was a decision which the family must make. This was significant in that it gave Karen back to her parents for this final decision about her care. This is not to say that the doctor couldn't have made this decision wisely, but rather that values were at stake here that clearly went beyond medicine.

Ideally, of course, it would be valuable to know Karen's wishes. Indeed, the patient's own wishes must be sought, if this is possible. But when this cannot ever be acquired, the proper *locus* for the decision is the family. My own addition to this would be to require that the attending physician say "when" this would be medically appropriate, for he has much greater training and experience in recognizing when a person is in the moribund state.

Dr. McIntyre's presentation provides specific insights by reference to the Quinlan case and through explication of ethical principles. His conclusions are not out of harmony with the *Declaration on Euthanasia.* What is most significant for our purposes is that he focuses on the terminally ill and does not deal with some of the other matters covered in the *Declaration,* such as defective infants, etc.

Two Roman Catholic clerics responded to the Questionnaire: The Rev. Joseph S. Battaglia, Director of the Department of Communications for the Archdiocese of Los Angeles, and Monsignor Thomas J. Woods, Charge d'Affaires of the Apostolic Nunciature, United States of America. Monsignor Woods pointed out that the *Declaration* does not use the term "passive euthanasia" to avoid "misunderstanding of its teaching." His answer to my survey question #1 was, "Yes, provided certain conditions are fulfilled." These conditions are "the ethical and theological grounds" provided in the *Declaration.* Both Father Battaglia and Monsignor Woods answered question #2 with "No" responses. The Monsignor referred to the *Declaration,* and Father Battaglia supported his "No" to the first part of the answer by stating:

It is the duty to preserve life. Even from a distance, to "provide" the wherewithal, the lethal dosage, would be active participation in the act. The direct intervention of anyone to purposefully take life cannot be sanctioned.

Concerning the second part of the question Father Battaglia wrote:

The individual does not have the *right* to ask anyone to assist in the administration of such actions. Expressed wishes cannot supplant the rights or duties of others to act in a moral manner.

Both clerics indicated that the Roman Catholic Church believes in a soul and afterlife, and in response to the query about the effect of euthanasia on the afterlife, Father Battaglia wrote:

The act would be seen as suicide. The presumption would be that the person could not be in his/her right mind. Consequently the act of suicide would not be a purposeful act. Supposedly the pain would be sufficient to render the individual "temporarily" unsettled. No judgment is made about the afterlife status.

Monsignor Woods referred to the *Declaration* teaching concerning "the gravity of rejecting God's sovereignty and loving plan, as also factors of diminished responsibility before His judgment and mercy."

Would the fact that death came by euthanasia affect the funeral rituals? Father Battaglia states that "There would be no penalty in the celebration of burial or funeral rituals" for the reasons he provided in the previous answer. Monsignor Woods preferred to change my term "would" to "could" in the questionnaire and noted that all would depend upon factors mentioned under the theme of "The Value of Human Life" in the *Declaration*. He also referred to the New Code of Canon Law, items 1184 and 1185.

Concerning counseling, Monsignor Woods suggested pastoral counseling in accordance with the *Declaration* with appropriate references to the Sacred Scripture. Father Battaglia stated that for "passive euthanasia" there would be "compassionate listening to the pain and suffering of the patient, an explanation of the principles involved, and prayer for the individual and family." So far as "active euthanasia" is concerned, Father Battaglia would engage in a "fully active attempt to dissuade from such a recourse, explanation of the view of the Church regarding such actions, and a judgment of the immoral nature of such actions."

THE VATICAN'S DECLARATION ON EUTHANASIA, 1980

INTRODUCTION

The rights and values pertaining to the human person occupy an important place among the questions discussed today. In this regard, the Second Vatican Ecumenical Council solemnly reaffirmed the lofty dignity of the human person, and in a special way his or her right to life. The Council therefore condemned crimes against life "such as any type of murder, genocide, abortion, euthanasia, or wilful suicide" (Pastoral Constitution *Gaudium et Spes*, 27).

More recently, the Sacred Congregation for the Doctrine of the Faith has reminded all the faithful of Catholic teaching on procured abortion.[1] The Congregation now considers it opportune to set forth the church's teaching on euthanasia.

It is indeed true that, in this sphere of teaching, the recent Popes have explained the principles, and these retain their full force;[2] but the progress of medical science in recent years has brought to the fore new aspects of the question of euthanasia, and these aspects call for further elucidation on the ethical level.

In modern society, in which even the fundamental values of human life are often called into question, cultural change exercises an influence upon the way of looking at suffering and death; moreover, medicine has increased its capacity to cure and to prolong life in particular circumstances, which sometimes give rise to moral problems. Thus people living in this situation experience no little anxiety about the meaning of advanced old age and death. They also begin to wonder whether they have the right to obtain for themselves or their fellowmen an "easy death", which would shorten suffering and which seems to them more in harmony with human dignity.

A number of Episcopal Conferences have raised questions on this subject with the Sacred Congregation for the Doctrine of the

Faith. The Congregation, having sought the opinion of experts on the various aspects of euthanasia, now wishes to respond to the Bishops' questions with the present Declaration, in order to help them to give correct teaching to the faithful entrusted to their care, and to offer them elements for reflection that they can present to the civil authorities with regard to this very serious matter.

The considerations set forth in the present document concern in the first place all those who place their faith and hope in Christ, who, through his life, death and Resurrection, has given a new meaning to existence and especially to the death of the Christian, as Saint Paul says: "If we live, we live to the Lord, and if we die, we die to the Lord" (*Rom* 14:8; cf. *Phil* 1:20).

As for those who profess other religions, many will agree with us that faith in God the Creator, Provider and Lord of life—if they share this belief—confers a lofty dignity upon every human person and guarantees respect for him or her.

It is hoped that this Declaration will meet with the approval of many people of good will, who, philosophical or ideological differences notwithstanding, have nevertheless a lively awareness of the rights of the human person. These rights have often in fact been proclaimed in recent years through declarations issued by International Congresses;[3] and since it is a question here of fundamental rights inherent in every human person, it is obviously wrong to have recourse to arguments from political pluralism or religious freedom in order to deny the universal value of those rights.

I

THE VALUE OF HUMAN LIFE

Human life is the basis of all goods, and is the necessary source and condition of every human activity and of all society. Most people regard life as something sacred and hold that no one may dispose of it at will, but believers see in life something greater, namely a gift of God's love, which they are called upon to preserve and make fruitful. And it is this latter consideration that gives rise to the following consequences:

1. No one can make an attempt on the life of an innocent person without opposing God's love for that person, without violating a fundamental right, and therefore without committing a crime of the utmost gravity.[4]

2. Everyone has the duty to lead his or her life in accordance with God's plan. That life is entrusted to the individual as a good that must bear fruit already here on earth, but that finds its full perfection only in eternal life.

3. Intentionally causing one's own death, or suicide, is therefore equally as wrong as murder; such an action on the part of a person is to be considered as a rejection of God's sovereignty and loving plan. Furthermore, suicide is also often a refusal of love for self, the denial of the natural instinct to live, a flight from the duties of justice and charity owed to one's neighbour, to various communities or to the whole of society—although, as is generally recognized, at times there are psychological factors present that can diminish responsibility or even completely remove it.

However, one must clearly distinguish suicide from that sacrifice of one's life whereby for a higher cause, such as God's glory, the salvation of souls or the service of one's brethren, a person offers his or her own life or puts it in danger (cf. *Jn* 15:14).

II
EUTHANASIA

In order that the question of euthanasia can be properly dealt with, it is first necessary to define the words used.

Etymologically speaking, in ancient times *euthanasia* meant an *easy death* without severe suffering. Today one no longer thinks of this original meaning of the word, but rather of some intervention of medicine whereby the sufferings of sickness or of the final agony are reduced, sometimes also with the danger of suppressing life prematurely. Ultimately, the word *euthanasia* is used in a more particular sense to mean "mercy killing", for the purpose of putting an end to extreme suffering, or saving abnormal babies, the mentally ill or the incurably sick from the prolongation, perhaps for many years, of a miserable life, which could impose too heavy a burden on their families or on society.

It is therefore necessary to state clearly in what sense the word is used in the present document.

By euthanasia is understood an action or an omission which of itself or by intention causes death, in order that all suffering may in this way be eliminated. Euthanasia's terms of reference, therefore, are to be found in the intention of the will and in the methods used.

It is necessary to state firmly once more that nothing and no one can in any way permit the killing of an innocent human being, whether a foetus or an embryo, an infant or an adult, an old person, or one suffering from an incurable disease, or a person who is dying. Furthermore, no one is permitted to ask for this act of killing, either for himself or herself or for another person entrusted to his or her care, nor can he or she consent to it, either explicitly or implicitly. Nor can any authority legitimately recommend or permit such an action. For it is a question of the violation of the divine law, an offence against the dignity of the human person, a crime against life, and an attack on humanity.

It may happen that, by reason of prolonged and barely tolerable pain, for deeply personal or other reasons, people may be led to believe that they can legitimately ask for death or obtain it for others. Although in these cases the guilt of the individual may be reduced or completely absent, nevertheless the error of judgment into which the conscience falls, perhaps in good faith, does not change the nature of this act of killing, which will always be in itself something to be rejected. The pleas of gravely ill people who sometimes ask for death are not to be understood as implying a true desire for euthanasia; in fact it is almost always a case of an anguished plea for help and love. What a sick person needs, besides medical care, is love, the human and supernatural warmth with which the sick person can and ought to be surrounded by all those close to him or her, parents and children, doctors and nurses.

III

THE MEANING OF SUFFERING FOR CHRISTIANS
AND THE USE OF PAINKILLERS

Death does not always come in dramatic circumstances after barely tolerable sufferings. Nor do we have to think only of extreme cases. Numerous testimonies which confirm one another lead one to the conclusion that nature itself has made provision to render more bearable at the moment of death separations that would be terribly painful to a person in full health. Hence it is that a prolonged illness, advanced old age, or a state of loneliness or neglect can bring about psychological conditions that facilitate the acceptance of death.

Nevertheless the fact remains that death, often preceded or accompanied by severe and prolonged suffering, is something which naturally causes people anguish.

Physical suffering is certainly an unavoidable element of the human condition; on the biological level, it constitutes a warning of which no one denies the usefulness; but, since it affects the human psychological makeup, it often exceeds its own biological usefulness and so can become so severe as to cause the desire to remove it at any cost.

According to Christian teaching, however, suffering, especially suffering during the last moments of life, has a special place in God's saving plan; it is in fact a sharing in Christ's Passion and a union with the redeeming sacrifice which he offered in obedience to the Father's will. Therefore one must not be surprised if some Christians prefer to moderate their use of painkillers, in order to accept voluntarily at least a part of their sufferings and thus associate themselves in a conscious way with the sufferings of Christ crucified (cf. *Mt* 27:34). Nevertheless it would be imprudent to impose a heroic way of acting as a general rule. On the contrary, human and Christian prudence suggest for the majority of sick people the use of medicines capable of alleviating or suppressing pain, even though these may cause as a secondary effect semiconsciousness and reduced lucidity. As for those who are not in a state to express themselves, one can reasonably presume that they wish to take these painkillers, and have them administered according to the doctor's advice.

But the intensive use of painkillers is not without difficulties, because the phenomenon of habituation generally makes it necessary to increase their dosage in order to maintain their efficacy. At this point it is fitting to recall a declaration by Pius XII, which retains its full force; in answer to a group of doctors who had put the question: "Is the suppression of pain and consciousness by the use of narcotics . . . permitted by religion and morality to the doctor and the patient (even at the approach of death and if one foresees that the use of narcotics will shorten life)?", the Pope said: "If no other means exist, and if, in the given circumstances, this does not prevent the carrying out of other religious and moral duties: Yes".[5] In this case, of course, death is in no way intended or sought, even if the risk of it is reasonably taken; the intention is simply to relieve pain effectively, using for this purpose painkillers available to medicine.

However, painkillers that cause unconsciousness need special consideration. For a person not only has to be able to satisfy his or her moral duties and family obligations; he or she also has to prepare himself or herself with full consciousness for meeting Christ. Thus Pius XII warns: "It is not right to deprive the dying person of consciousness without a serious reason".[6]

IV
DUE PROPORTION IN THE USE OF REMEDIES

Today it is very important to protect, at the moment of death, both the dignity of the human person and the Christian concept of life, against a technological attitude that threatens to become an abuse. Thus, some people speak of a "right to die", which is an expression that does not mean the right to procure death either by one's own hand or by means of someone else, as one pleases, but rather the right to die peacefully with human and Christian dignity. From this point of view, the use of therapeutic means can sometimes pose problems.

In numerous cases, the complexity of the situation can be such as to cause doubts about the way ethical principles should be applied. In the final analysis, it pertains to the conscience either of the sick person, or of those qualified to speak in the sick person's name, or of the doctors, to decide, in the light of moral obligations and of the various aspects of the case.

Everyone has the duty to care for his or her own health or to seek such care from others. Those whose task it is to care for the sick must do so conscientiously and administer the remedies that seem necessary or useful.

However, is it necessary in all circumstances to have recourse to all possible remedies?

In the past, moralists replied that one is never obliged to use "extraordinary" means. This reply, which as a principle still holds good, is perhaps less clear today, by reason of the imprecision of the term and the rapid progress made in the treatment of sickness. Thus some people prefer to speak of "proportionate" and "disproportionate" means. In any case, it will be possible to make a correct judgment as to the means by studying the type of treatment to be used, its degree of complexity or risk, its cost and the possibilities of using it, and comparing these elements with the result that can be expected, taking into account the state of the sick person and his or her physical and moral resources.

In order to facilitate the application of these general principles, the following clarifications can be added:

> If there are no other sufficient remedies, it is permitted, with the patient's consent, to have recourse to the means provided by the most advanced medical techniques, even if these means are still at the experimental stage and are not without a certain risk. By accepting them, the patient can even show generosity in the service of humanity.

> It is also permitted, with the patient's consent, to interrupt these means, where the results fall short of expectations. But for such a decision to be made, account will have to be taken of the reasonable wishes of the patient and the patient's family, as also

of the advice of the doctors who are specially competent in the matter. The latter may in particular judge that the investment in instruments and personnel is disproportionate to the results foreseen; they may also judge that the techniques applied impose on the patient strain or suffering out of proportion with the benefits which he or she may gain from such techniques.

It is also permissible to make do with the normal means that medicine can offer. Therefore one cannot impose on anyone the obligation to have recourse to a technique which is already in use but which carries a risk or is burdensome. Such a refusal is not the equivalent of suicide; on the contrary, it should be considered as an acceptance of the human condition, or a wish to avoid the application of a medical procedure disproportionate to the results that can be expected, or a desire not to impose excessive expense on the family or the community.

When inevitable death is imminent in spite of the means used, it is permitted in conscience to take the decision to refuse forms of treatment that would only secure a precarious and burdensome prolongation of life, so long as the normal care due to the sick person in similar cases is not interrupted. In such circumstances the doctor has no reason to reproach himself with failing to help the person in danger.

CONCLUSION

The norms contained in the present Declaration are inspired by a profound desire to serve people in accordance with the plan of the Creator. Life is a gift of God, and on the other hand death is unavoidable; it is necessary therefore that we, without in any way hastening the hour of death, should be able to accept it with full responsibility and dignity. It is true that death marks the end of our earthly existence, but at the same time it opens the door to immortal life. Therefore all must prepare themselves for this event in the light of human values, and Christians even more so in the light of faith.

As for those who work in the medical profession, they ought to neglect no means of making all their skill available to the sick and the dying; but they should also remember how much more necessary it is to provide them with the comfort of boundless kindness and heartfelt charity. Such service to people is also service to Christ the Lord, who said: "As you did it to one of the least of these my brethren, you did it to me" (*Mt* 25: 40).

At the audience granted to the undersigned Prefect, His Holiness Pope John Paul II approved this Declaration, adopted at the ordinary meeting of the Sacred Congregation for the Doctrine of the Faith, and ordered its publication.

Rome, the Sacred Congregation for the Doctrine of the Faith, 5 May 1980.

Franjo Card. Šeper
Prefect

† Jérôme Hamer, O. P.
Tit. Archbishop of Lorium
Secretary

N O T E S

1. *Declaration on Procured Abortion*, 18 November 1974: *AAS* 66 (1974), pp. 730–747.

2. Pius XII, *Address to those attending the Congress of the International Union of Catholic Women's Leagues*, 11 September 1947: *AAS* 39 (1947), p. 483; *Address to the Italian Catholic Union of Midwives*, 29 October 1951: *AAS* 43 (1951), pp. 835–854; *Speech to the members of the International Office of military medicine documentation*, 19 October 1953: *AAS* 45 (1953), pp. 744–754; *Address to those taking part in the IXth Congress of the Italian Anaesthesiological Society*, 24 February 1957: *AAS* 49 (1957), p. 146; cf. also *Address on "reanimation"* 24 November 1957: *AAS* 49 (1957), pp. 1027–1033; Paul VI, *Address to the members of the United Nations Special Committee on Apartheid*, 22 May 1974: *AAS* 66 (1974), p. 346; John Paul II: *Address to the Bishops of the United States of America*, 5 October 1979: *AAS* 71 (1979), p. 1225.

3. One thinks especially of Recommendation 779 (1976) on the rights of the sick and dying, of the Parliamentary Assembly of the Council of Europe at its XXVIIth Ordinary Session; cf. SIPECA, No. 1, March 1977, pp. 14–15.

4. We leave aside completely the problems of the death penalty and of war, which involve specific considerations that do not concern the present subject.

5. PIUS XII, *Address* of 24 February 1957: *AAS* 49 (1957), p. 147.

6. PIUS XII, *ibid.,* p. 145; cf. *Address* of 9 September 1958: *AAS* 50 (1958), p. 694.

The Greek
Orthodox Church

The Rev. Stanley S. Harakas is Professor of Orthodox Christian Ethics at the Holy Cross Greek Orthodox School of Theology and the author of *Contemporary Moral Issues* (Light and Life Publishing Company, 1982). In his response to the questionnaire, Professor Harakas warns, "It should be made very clear that these responses, though they reflect the mind and the sense of the Orthodox Church in general, cannot be understood as official, but that they do in some way come to a reflection of the official position of the Orthodox Church."

Professor Harakas believes that:

> . . . the Orthodox Church would sanction the removal of the life-support system. The reason for this is that K. is already dead. The machines are simply keeping the dead body "functioning." That makes clear the ethical and the theological grounds. Our church simply would not want to see the inordinate continuation of biological function after the person is dead. We would make that judgment on the basis of the physician's opinion that the brain is "gone."

The Orthodox Church would not sanction active euthanasia, which Professor Harakas notes is "correctly identified as suicide" (in the questionnaire). He writes:

45

There is clear canonical teaching in the Orthodox Church and moral teachings that prohibits taking of life in this fashion. This would simply be self-murder and would be understood as sin since it violates the commandment that we are not to murder or kill.

Nor would the Orthodox Church sanction assisted suicide: "This is essentially an act of murder." And even should M. request help, "Our Church would clearly identify this as homicide or murder or even compassionate murder, if such a term is admissible, but it would be something violated by the fundamental moral code 'Thou shalt not murder.'"

In Orthodox thinking (which accepts a belief in a soul, afterlife and divine judgment), because active euthanasia would be considered suicide, "The person who committed this act would not have a chance to repent of a very serious sin. It would probably mean eternal condemnation." Burial rituals might also be affected. "If the act of 'active' euthanasia were understood clearly as an act of suicide, the church cannot by Canon Law bury the individual, unless it is shown through competent medical certification that the person was mentally ill in doing the act. The chance is that a person who had announced previously the intention to commit 'active' euthanasia would not be buried from the church."

In response to the 5th question pertaining to passive euthanasia Professor Harakas wrote, "In reference to so-called 'passive' euthanasia, allowing to die, our publications indicate that this is not an appropriate thing to do, especially if it is done in council with the family and the priest. Under 'active' euthanasia as indicated, it would be considered a form of suicide and therefore would be condemned, and persons would be urged not to do such a thing."

Some dimensions of the theological and biblical bases for the Greek Orthodox position are provided in Professor Harakas' book *Contemporary Moral Issues*. He recognizes changes in the ways in which persons view death and dying and provides information concerning "The Traditional View" and "The Orthodox Response" (pp. 166ff):

The Traditional View

The traditional view in Western Civilization is that death is an enemy, an evil which is resented, fought against and battled, even though it is seen as inevitable. Death is darkness. It is the end of life on earth as we know it. It is the conclusion of our efforts, our hopes, our dreams, our expectations, our existence as earth-borne beings. That is why, considered in itself, death is evil. The Fourth Horseman of the Apocalypse is a powerful biblical symbol of the evil of death.

"And I saw, and behold, a pale horse, and its rider's name was Death, and Hades followed him; and they were given power over a fourth of the earth, to kill with a sword and with famine and with pestilence and by wild beasts of the earth" (Revelation 6:8).

That is why St. Paul could write, without threat of opposition, that "the last enemy to be destroyed is death" (1 Cor. 15:26).

But death is one thing and dying is another. In the experience of dying, dying is conceived as a different kind of process, depending on the overall view of life which we may have. In history, dying and its meaning are conditioned by the way we respond to the fact of death. It was Freud who said, "The goal of all life is death."

There are three basic responses to death which have served to dictate how we die. The first is fear. This is the view which dominates the thinking about dying in history. Death is recognized as the end, the tragedy that it is, and people approach the end with the agony of self-extinction. They battle it with a fierce clinging to life, in spite of its unavoidability.

The second basic response to death belonged in the past to a small group of philosophers. Epicurus rationalized death out of existence: "Thus that which is the most awful of evils, death, is nothing to us, since when we exist, there is no death, and when there is death, we do not exist."

The philosopher and essayist Montaigne continued this tradition of whistling in the dark by saying it even more sharply. "Of all the benefits which virtue confers upon us, the contempt of death is one of the greatest." Contempt for death makes dying appear easier. For then it is as if it is nothing—not enemy, not tragedy, not pain, not suffering. Consequently, it is a non-thing which is neither to be feared, respected, nor regarded.

The Orthodox Response

The third basic response is the Christian response. Orthodox Christianity—unlike Western Christianity—does not view physical death as a natural result of living. Rather, because death is the consequence of humanity's sin, it is not natural to us. For Orthodoxy, death in its ultimate sense is a perversion of our nature: it is a destructive extension of sin in our lives. "Therefore, as sin came into the world through one man, and death through sin, and so death spread to all men because all men sinned . . . " (Romans 5:12).

Yet, Christians hold also that the power of death over us has been destroyed, essentially, by the saving work of Jesus Christ. Thus, even though death continues to be evil, dying takes on new meaning. The Christian no longer fears dying, even though death is a fearsome thing. He knows and trusts in "our Saviour, Christ Jesus, who abolished death and brought life and immortality to light through the gospel" (1 Timothy 1:10). Together with Saint Paul, every Christian facing his or her own death can repeat the words of the Prophet Isaiah, "Death is swallowed up in victory," as well as the words of Prophet Hosea, "O death, where is thy victory? O death, where is thy sting?" (1 Corinthians 15:55–56). The Christian knows the evil and the tragedy of death, but meets and overcomes it through sharing in the resurrected Christ's victory over death.

In discussing the issue of "the Right to Die," Professor Harakas notes that although the Orthodox Christian tradition does not provide specific guidance, "We have several basic ethical traditions in Orthodoxy upon which we are able to draw." These are (pp. 171 f):

The first is that God is the author of life and that we have the responsibility to defend, protect and enhance life as a basis for living God's will. God is the giver of life, and "in his hand is the life of every living thing and the breath of all mankind" (Job 12:10). To wrongfully take the life of an innocent person is murder and is condemned as a sin (Exodus 20:13).

On the other hand, "it is appointed for men to die once" (Hebrew 9:27). Physical death is inevitable, yet it is something which comes normally *in spite* of our efforts to preserve life. There is something which rings of the barbaric in calls for the "elimination" of human life. That is why *the Orthodox Church completely and unalterably opposes euthanasia*. It is a fearful and dangerous "playing at God" by fallible human beings.

But modern medicine has perhaps gone to the other extreme. It is able now to "preserve" lives which God struggles to take! The various substitute organs devised by medical science are good and useful as therapeutic means. When, for instance, an artificial lung or an artificial kidney is used during an operation, it permits treatment of the diseased natural organ by the surgeon. Often these artificial mechanical organs are used over a period of time so that the patient's life is maintained while the weakened organism is allowed time and energy to recuperate. Sometimes, such as with kidney machines and artificial lungs, almost permanent use of the machine is required. In all these cases, life is enhanced and preserved. Normally speaking, the use of such methods is a necessary and useful step in the therapeutic process whose goal is the restoration of health and life.

When the time comes that the bodily functions do break down completely and irrevocably, and machines continue to keep "a dead body functioning as if it were alive," then, "The Church holds that there comes a time to die." Indeed there is a service (in the prayer book) designed for this very situation. When ordinary medical efforts are incapable of sustaining life, and when the body literally struggles to die, the Church prays as follows:

> . . . *Thou has commanded the dissolution of the indescribable bond of soul and body, O God of Spirits, and has ordered them to be separated by Thy divine will. The body is thus to be returned to the elements from which it was made, and the soul is to proceed to the source of its existence, until the resurrection of all. For this reason we implore Thee, the eternal and immortal Father, the Only-begotten Son and the All-Holy Spirit, that Thou bring about the peaceful separation of the soul of Thy servant (name) from his/her body.*

In such a situation there are "clear Orthodox Christian guidelines" available. They are as follows:

1. We have the responsibility, as a trust from God, to maintain, preserve and protect our own lives and those lives entrusted to us;

2. In case of illness, we are obligated to use every method available to us to restore health, both spiritual and medical;
3. Life is so precious and to be so respected that even when health cannot be fully restored, it should be protected and maintained;
4. When, however, the major physical systems have broken down, and there does not seem to be any reasonable expectation that they can be restored, Orthodox Christians may properly allow extraordinary mechanical devices to be removed. When the body is struggling to die, when its numerous physical systems break down, when it cannot be reasonably expected that the bodily systems will be able to regain their potential for life, the Orthodox Christian is no longer obligated to continue the use of extraordinary mechanical devices;
5. The decision should never be taken alone. It should be shared by the family, if possible. And, certainly, it should be made on the basis of expert medical opinion in consultation with the physician in charge of the case. It should also be made with the advice, counsel and prayer of the priest.

This action should never be confused with euthanasia, which brings to an end, deliberately and consciously, a life which is capable of maintaining itself with normal care. It is one thing to kill and murder; it is quite another to "allow the peaceful separation of soul and body."

But Greek Orthodoxy is not out of touch with modern dilemmas, and euthanasia must be considered. Here Professor Harakas looks at the teachings of the Church fathers, provides some guidelines for the present, and leaves the question open as far as the future is concerned. He writes (pp. 174ff):

A partial answer to this question is to be found in the Orthodox perspective of death. The fathers tell us that death is an unnatural wrenching of the soul from the body leading to the destruction of the psycho-somatic unity that constitutes the human person. Here man is a microcosm, uniting in himself the material and spiritual realms of God's creation. In addition, he bears the imprint of image and likeness to God, and in this resemblance, Adam, the first man, enjoyed immortality. But through the Fall man rejected God, the only source of authentic life, destroying the likeness and fracturing the image. He strove to make his own life apart from God and, thus, chose death.

Nevertheless, God did not desire that His creation remain in its fallen state, and in His great mercy, He sent His beloved Son into the world to transform and unite all things in Himself. By His Life, Death, and Resurrection, Christ Jesus restored the image and likeness in man to its original wholeness. All aspects of human existence were thereby transformed including death which through the Resurrection has become a passage into eternal life.

As a consequence, Christians should cherish their life on this earth as a most precious gift from God entrusted to them for a time, never forgetting that this life has been bought with a price and already been made new in Christ. At the same time, we must accept the inevitability of our physical death, not in despair, but with anticipation of the Last Day when we shall all be raised up in a transfigured flesh.

A further inference from this conception of life and death is that we do not deliberately contribute to the death of others. Therefore, euthanasia being a deliberate taking of human life, does not constitute a viable alternative for the Orthodox physician or patient.

Some Guidelines

While the Church suffers with those who are grave distress, she cannot so betray her commitment to the preservation of human life. Yet, the Church is not insensitive to the needs of those who suffer and in its concern stresses the Christian obligation to relieve pain and make the patient as comfortable as possible. The use of pain killers, such as morphine, is permissible; where they may constitute an undefined effect on the length of the patient's life, no serious attention need be given, when the motive is the comfort and over-all well-being of the patient.

Those experiencing great physical pain are also reminded that even suffering has acquired new meaning by our Lord's own passion and has become a means to an enhanced communion with God and an opportunity for spiritual growth.

At the same time, the Orthodox Church parts with those members of the medical profession and others who refuse to acknowledge the inevitability of physical death and advocate the use of "extraordinary measures", at whatever material and psychological cost, to keep a patient alive when there is no hope of restoration to a meaningful, functional existence. The Church which prays for the "quick and painless death" (Prayer for the Separation of Soul and Body) of the terminally-ill patient, considers this kind of treatment not only a poor use of scarce medical resources, but a denial of the will of God.

We must remember, of course, that there are no final, clear-cut answers: today's "extraordinary measures" fast become tomorrow's regular life-saving procedures. And any life-death decisions to withhold treatment must be considered on an individual case by case basis in consultation with the patient or his next of kin, his physician and spiritual advisor.

He summarizes the Church's position as follows:

The Church, therefore, distinguishes between euthanasia and the withholding of extraordinary means to prolong life unable to sustain itself. It affirms the sanctity of human life and man's God-given responsibility to preserve life. But it rejects an attitude which disregards the inevitability of physical death. The only "good death" for the Orthodox Christian is the peaceful acceptance of the end of his or her earthly life with faith and trust in God and the promise of the Resurrection.

On May 15th, 1984, Father Harakas participated in a Medical Ethics Symposium at Booth Memorial Medical Center in Flushing, New York. Father Harakas' panel comments were titled "The Terminally Ill: Morality, Economics, Physician's Responsibility." He proposed certain guidelines for ethical decision-making concerning the care of the terminally ill, which included the traditional belief "that active life-taking of the innocent is immoral and that active taking of one's own life is wrong . . . that life itself is one of the supreme values, that death is evil and that, by and large, that which promotes life and staves off death is good." Further, he adds that "the intrinsic value of each person" is a primary value. He expressed concern that ignoring of traditional values might have a negative effect on "the self-understanding of the medical profession . . . as the chief healing agent in our society." Indeed, "the abandonment of therapeutic efforts for the terminally ill may well foster such a utilitarian approach to life itself that it will provide a 'wedge' which will undermine the respect for the human dignity of persons, precisely in the name of so-called 'death with dignity.'"

In conclusion, Professor Harakas provided some guidelines for the approach to the question of the treatment of the terminally ill:

1. Basically, all persons, including the patient, the family, society as a whole, and the medical community ought to function within a fundamental bias toward the protection and conservation of life, and to function in ways which restrict and limit death. For the physician, this necessarily means that the traditional bias toward healing and therapy must remain primary.
2. In facing illness, we are obligated to use every method available to us to restore health. The principle that life is so precious that it is to be respected and cared for even when health cannot be fully restored should be protected and maintained as ethically valid.
3. When, however, the major physical systems have broken down, and there does not seem to be any reasonable expectation that they can be restored, that is, when over-arching evidence supports a prognosis that the patient is terminally ill, the practitioner, the individual patient, the family and all others associated with the situation are not morally obligated, and ought not to feel obligated, to expend energy, time and resources in a misdirected effort to fend off death.
4. The moral responsibility then changes in this measure: That the concern for the alleviation of pain and suffering, and the personal dimensions of the patient's life receive primary attention. This means that there is a change in moral priorities. For the physician and the medical team, the concern for the broadly understood personal life of the patient assumes the central place, and the medical efforts assume the character of care, rather than therapy.
5. In a sense, this also addresses the issue of the expenditure of money. The expenditure of money on unnecessary and inappropriate therapeutic efforts in order to convince self, family, legal community, or medical peers that "we are doing everything possible" is morally unfitting. On the other hand, the expenditure of money to provide "a good dying" is both appropriate and fitting and ethically indicated. Ethically speaking, of course, there is the question of proportionality. But, by and large, it does not seem to me that the *amount* of money spent is the critical factor. The moral responsibility remains, in any case. Were it, for example, cheaper to actively seek therapy for the terminally ill patient, than to provide the appropriate care required for a "good death," it still would not be right to do it.

6. Finally, it should be emphasized, that nothing indicated in what has been said above permits or advocates the active taking of a human life, even when it is experiencing terminal illness. Rather, just the opposite. A terminally ill person remains a person, within a family, part of the human race, a child of God. Active taking of a life in such a case continues to fly in the face of the moral bias for the protection and continuation of life whether it be done by another person, on his or her initiative, or on the initiative of the terminally ill person.

The Russian
Orthodox Church

Professor Thomas Hopko, of St. Vladimir's Seminary of the Orthodox Church in America, responded to the questionnaire on behalf of the Russian Orthodox Church, and the Very Reverend Archpriest A. Mileant of the Protection of the Holy Virgin Russian Orthodox Church in Los Angeles, wrote a letter that covered some of the issues.

Professor Hopko wrote in reply to the first question:

> I believe that we *would* allow for removal of the system in such a case, if the family would want it and agree, and be able spiritually to handle it. We do not find it ethically imperative to keep certain bodily functions acting when a person cannot recover.

The Rev. Father Mileant commented, "We consider that human life is a gift of God, which no one has the right to forcibly take away; however, in our teaching it is not necessary to take 'heroic' measures to prolong the life of a terminally ill patient; in this case, we leave the decision to God who gives life and permits illness."

The Church does not sanction active euthanasia. Father Mileant wrote, " . . . if a person is in great pain and requests to be allowed to die sooner (or his relatives so request), we do not consider it possible to accede to his request, because we believe that suffering is often sent by God for the remission of our sins and the salvation

55

of our souls; so if God has sent someone pain which cannot be alleviated by normal means (pain-killer shots, etc.), we must resign ourselves in the knowledge that this pain is necessary and inevitable." Professor Hopko wrote in response to the second question and the case of M. described there:

> Here we say that the person must, and with God's help can, bear what needs to be borne, and in so doing, will give glory to God and encouragement and inspiration to others. No one has the right to take their life in a direct, active manner. The "active struggle" in our view is critically important. People vary greatly in what they consider to be "unbearable." Suicide is no answer.

Indeed, assisted suicide or any form of what is labeled in the questionnaire as "compassionate murder" is eschewed because "It would be a crime and a sin."

The Russian Orthodox Church believes in a soul, in afterlife and in divine judgment. Professor Hopko states, "We believe the person will answer to God and his fellow creatures for actions done in this life. The refusal of life here leads to the conclusion that 'life' would be rejected 'there.' It is not the case of God punishing people for what they have done, as much as the 'immanent punishment' inherent in the evil act, with the concurrent rejection of God's mercy and forgiveness for if there is no 'wrong' there is no need for mercy."

Father Mileant expanded on these ideas:

> Concerning the life beyond, we firmly believe that a person has an immortal soul. After his death, his body dissolves, but the soul continues to think, feel and move, as it did in his earthly life.
>
> We believe in only two conditions of the soul, or rather two places where the souls go after death, depending on God's decision; these two places are heaven and hell. We do not admit a medium condition, or purgatory, as in the Roman Catholic faith. We consider it to be a human invention. Nothing is said about it by the Fathers of the Church antiquity, or in the Bible; our Lord Jesus Christ also said nothing about it. We believe what is said in the Holy Scriptures, i.e., the existence of heaven and hell; and only God has the authority to imprison a person in hell or take him out of it.

We also do not admit that a soul sent by God to hell will always remain there. We admit that a soul can be liberated from hell by God's mercy, by the prayers of the Church, or by the good deeds performed in his memory by his relatives and friends. However, we do not know who will be saved and who will be condemned; only God has that knowledge of human souls; we therefore pray both for the righteous (they may have some sins we do not know about) and for the sinners (as God may know of some good deeds of theirs that are unknown to us). For this reason we pray basically for all, and firmly believe in the great power of Church prayers.

Distinction is made in the funeral rituals for those who end their own lives. "If the person himself *willed* death and participated in it consciously," Professor Hopko wrote, "we *do* have a service, but it is brief and not the one for whom 'God has taken.'"

Concerning counseling by the Church, Professor Hopko commented:

We would try to determine if really, barring a miracle (which can happen with or without the system), the person would not recover and is *merely* not even being kept "alive" but kept with certain bodily functions activated—and would counsel to allow nature to take its course, hoping to remove any feelings of guilt on the part of those deciding to "pull the plug."

If active euthanasia was being contemplated, he stated that here they would "try to help the person to believe that their struggle and pain has meaning—for themselves and others. The depth of the person's faith and convictions in a 'crucified God ' are crucial in the counseling approach."

The Episcopal Church

John K. Martin, Secretary for Communication of the Anglican Consultative Council, reviewed the copies of the reports of the Lambeth Conferences of the Anglican Church and concluded, "As far as I can see there are no statements on this subject (euthanasia)." He commented, "I do know, however, that a number of Churches who are members of the Anglican Communion have expressed their mind on this matter, if not through their synods, then through research and the engagement of their Boards for Social Responsibility."

The Rev. David Scott of the Protestant Episcopal Church wrote:

The Episcopal Church has not formulated and published any official position on the questions surrounding "euthanasia." Therefore, it is impossible to answer the questions as you formulate them, e.g., "would your religious organization sanction . . . " Your language . . . presupposes a kind of authority of theological teaching and writing which is not relevant in the Episcopal Church. The Episcopal Church has taken specific stands on, for example, abortion. These are published in the Journals of the General Convention of the Church. But even these "official" resolutions are not juridically binding on Episcopalians.

Mrs. G. Nancy Deppen, Consultant for Information and Resource at The Episcopal Church Center in New York, shared a statement reflecting opposition to euthanasia by the General Convention in 1982, which is taken from *Social Policy of the Episcopal Church in the Twentieth Century,* by Weston, under the theme of "Special Causes" (p. 56):

> Another single-occasion action was an expression of complete "opposition to the legalizing of the practice of Euthanasia, under any circumstances whatsoever" by the General Convention of 1952. The statement drew attention to: "a growing movement to legalize the practice of Euthanasia." It also asserted that " . . . this Church believes that as God gives life so only through the operation of the laws of nature can life rightly be taken from human beings." An editorial in *The Living Church,* more than a decade earlier, had vigorously opposed proposals to legalize the practice of Euthanasia. By contrast, however, another meeting of the General Convention tabled a resolution against capital punishment.

In the February 21, 1973, issue of *The Christian Century* Dr. Robert M. Cooper, who was at that time Assistant Professor of Ethics and Moral Theology at Nashotah House (Episcopal) in Nashotah, Wisconsin, wrote an article titled "Euthanasia and the Notion of 'Death with Dignity'" (pp. 225ff). He suggested that "the contemporary stress on euthanasia can be seen in part as evidence of our culture's pervasive concern for what is cosmetically pleasing . . . With this concern goes the belief (usually unstated) that pain— *physical* suffering, in this instance—is life's greatest evil."

Dr. Cooper argued that he found "the idea of dignity basically abstract and not particularly Christian." He continued:

> First, it is abstract because it operates on the assumption that we know what is a *fitting,* a *worthy* death for a human being, and because it ignores the specificity of the person and deals with him as one human instance under the generalizing concept of "dignity." More fundamental, especially for the Christian, is my second point. We do not yet fully know what it is to be human; and because we do not know, we cannot, or ought not, glibly speak of "human dignity." But most of us are arrogant enough to suppose that we know what is *human* being. Thus we talk readily about "humanizing the structures of government," "humanizing the educational system," etc. An article in the *Episcopalian*

(October 1972, p. 40) quotes Mrs. Henry J. Mali, president of the Euthanasia Educational Fund and the Euthanasia Society of America, as saying that the aim of both those organizations "is to humanize the treatment of terminal illness, so death may come gently." At the risk of appearing monstrous, I must comment that this view, while indeed *humanistic*, is not necessarily Christian. "Beloved," we read in the First Epistle of John (3:2, RSV), "we are God's children now; it does not yet appear what we shall be, but we know that when he appears we shall be like him, for we shall see him as he is." For Christians this verse does not function as a counsel of despair but rather as a keynote for reverence and hope. Our faith is that God has shown himself in his Christ, and that in the Christ we can begin to perceive God's idea of being human.

Dr. Cooper then considered the concept of human suffering. In particular, he referred to a statement he quoted earlier, by Mrs. Mali, "that death may come gently." He wrote:

This seems to imply that pain, suffering, is undignified. Is it? Clearly, some suffering is undignified, but some is not. Indeed, the bearing of pain is often noble. Christ's bearing of pain, however, takes on trans-cendent importance for mankind—or so Christian faith holds. Yet mul-titudes in our society insist that pain is the greatest evil in life; or, put the other way, that pleasure is the greatest good. There are probably those who hold that suffering or pain is the greatest evil who do not, in fact, hold its corollary, that pleasure is the greatest good. I submit that, in either form, this is the view that largely governs our culture and manifests itself everywhere—not least in the arguments of euthanasia.

But the Christian view is that suffering is fundamental to human being, whatever human being is or may turn out to be. The Christian view is that happiness is not the same as pleasure. It is possible to be happy while suffering pain. I think it was C. S. Lewis who pointed out that the martyr slowly burning to death on a griddle may be said to be happy, though it would be crazy to say that he is experiencing pleasure. Pain is not the greatest evil known to man, and pleasure is not his greatest good. Surely the evil greater than pain is to deny that pain, excruciating pain, is radically an ingredient of the human condition.

Of course Dr. Cooper's statements are his own, but they reflect some aspects of the dialogue that took place within the Episcopal Church concerning this issue. On December 18, 1976, Tom Lambert, staff writer for the *Los Angeles Times,* reported on an address given by the Most Rev. Donald Coggan, Archbishop of Canterbury, to the Royal Society of Medicine, and on the responses to the address. The article read, in part:

> The Most Rev. Donald Coggan disputed "the view held by many that Christians believe that life must be artificially prolonged under all circumstances . . . just for the sake of doing so."
>
> Coggan quoted the 19th-century poet Arthur Clough: "Thou should not kill, but needst not strive officiously to keep alive."
>
> The London Times, Daily Mail and Daily Telegraph endorsed parts or all of the 67-year-old archbishop's speech, which presumably reflected the Church of England's views. It also was approved in varying degree by the British Medical Assn., Britain's Human Rights Assn. and the Voluntary Euthanasia Society.
>
> A spokesman for the euthanasia group said, however, that Coggan "does not go as far as we would." The archbishop had warned against legalized euthanasia, and suggested that the issue of a patient's life or death should be the responsibility of his doctors, clergymen and relatives.
>
> The archbishop also was praised editorially for deploring what he called "the conspiracy of silence" which he claimed cloaks the subject of death, and the "charade" in which a terminally ill person is told he is getting better.
>
> Objections were raised to his apparent suggestion that National Health Service doctors' life-death decisions also involve a "responsibility" to the government, the taxpayers and "other patients in the long waiting queue."
>
> "The resources of the national exchequer are not limitless, and the prolongation of the life of one aged patient may in fact entail the deprivation of aid to others and even the shortening of their lives," the archbishop said.
>
> President Sir Rodney Smith of Britain's Royal College of Surgeons described as "unacceptable" the archbishop's suggestion that doctors should consider "the problem of availability of resources" when treating terminally or incurably ill patients. "Knowledge and conscience" must guide the doctors, Smith said.

Mrs. Deppen provided a copy of a resolution passed at the General Convention, held in 1982, pertaining to the Uniform Determination of Death Act. The resolution stated:

> RESOLVED, that this Executive Council commends the President's Commission for the Study of Ethical Problems in Medicine, which was charged with developing a uniform determination of death statute; and be it further
>
> RESOLVED, that the report and position of this Commission be circulated throughout The Episcopal Church; and be it further
>
> RESOLVED, that Episcopalians be encouraged to consider and to comment on the proposed Uniform Determination of Death Act (U.D.D.A.):
>
> > "An individual who has sustained either 1) irreversible cessation of circulatory and respiratory functions, or 2) irreversible cessation of all functions of the entire brain, including brain stem, is dead. A determination of death must be made in accordance with accepted medical standards."

As the Rev. David Scott pointed out, such resolutions are not binding on Episcopalians. Therefore, it should be expected that the dialogue concerning euthanasia will continue.

The Lutheran Church

The Lutheran Church—Missouri Synod—is one American Church group that has actively been studying the relationship between faith and conduct as related to euthanasia. At the 1971 convention, in resolution 9-07, the Church affirmed its belief "that the world is God's creation" and "that human life is God's gift" and that, therefore, "human life must be treasured, supported and protected." The affirmations went on to state:

> We encourage all people to avoid perverting God's will by resorting to indiscriminate termination of life, either directly through such acts as abortion or euthanasia or indirectly through the improper use of drugs, tobacco, and alcohol, or any of God's means for sustaining life.

In 1975, the Convention was presented with Resolution 8-10, which never materialized "since it failed to receive action before adjournment." Because the motion was recorded in the Convention Proceedings, however, it did serve to alert the Lutheran membership of the continuing concern about euthanasia. The resolution read, in part:

> WHEREAS, God created men in His image and gave them life; and
> WHEREAS, The world belittles the value of human life through perverting God's will by prematurely terminating life through such acts as indiscriminate abortion, euthanasia, and the improper use of drugs, tobacco, and alcohol . . .

(It should be noted that, "In Session 7 the committee deleted 'indiscriminate' before 'euthanasia'.")

At the 1977 Convention, a resolution "To Affirm the Sacredness of Human Life" (3–30) was formally adopted. It read:

> WHEREAS, Life is a gift from God and comes into being by an act that shares in the creative powers of God Himself; and
>
> WHEREAS, Scripture teaches that suffering has a purposes of God; and
>
> WHEREAS, Life and death belong in the realm of God's providence; and
>
> WHEREAS, Scripture teaches that suffering has a positive purpose and value in God's economy and is not to be avoided at all costs (2 Cor. 1:5–7; 2 Cor. 4:7–11; Heb. 12:5–11; Rom. 8:16–18, 28, 35–39; Phil. 3:10; Col. 1:24); and
>
> WHEREAS, We sing of the positive purpose of suffering in our worship (*TLH*, 523, 528, 533, et al.); and
>
> WHEREAS, The Commission on Theology and Church Relations (CTCR) and its Social Concerns Committee (SCC) currently have a study in progress regarding the question of euthanasia; and
>
> WHEREAS, The willful taking of the life of one human being by another is contrary to the Word and will of God (Ex. 20:13); therefore be it
>
> RESOLVED, That the Synod affirm that human life is sacred and finds meaning and purpose in seeking and following God's will, not in self-centered pleasure, a concern for convenience, or a desire for comfort; and be it further
>
> RESOLVED, That the Synod affirm the positive benefits of suffering, so that God's children may be comforted in Christ Jesus and have their sights focused more firmly on eternal values; and be it further
>
> RESOLVED, That the Synod unequivocally declare that the practice known as euthanasia, namely, inducing death, is contrary to God's Word and will and cannot be condoned or justified; and be it finally
>
> RESOLVED, That the CTCR and its SCC be urged to complete their study as soon as possible.

In October 1979, the Commission on Theology and Church Relations published the "Report on Euthanasia with Guiding Principles" which had been prepared by its Social Concerns Committee (referred to in the 1977 resolution 3-30). This very thorough study opened with a definition of euthanasia which made a distinction between active and passive forms. Active euthanasia was defined as "taking direct steps to end the life of persons who are not necessarily dying, but who, in the opinion of some, are better off dead. It is also described as the deliberate easing into death of a patient suffering from a painful or fatal disease." Passive euthanasia is "the discontinuance or avoidance of extraordinary means of preserving life when there is no prospect of recovery."

But, the report continues, "This practice does not, in a proper medical sense, signify euthanasia. Instead, it normally belongs to the responsible care that medical personnel exhibit toward patients that appear to have irrevocably entered the process of dying." The report refers to specific cases, and as support for clearly separating "euthanasia" from "responsible care" noted:

> Other examples of situations which are said to call for euthanasia involve persons suffering from unresponsive, far-advanced cancer with intractable pain, irreversible brain damage resulting in a vegetative state, and individuals with marked senility who suffer from life-threatening illnesses. It is to exceptional cases of this kind that the following statement of the New York Academy of Medicine applies:
>
> > When, in the opinion of the attending physicians, measures to prolong life in which no realistic hope of effecting significant improvement will cause further pain and suffering to the patient and family, we support conservative passive medical care in place of heroic measures in the management of a patient afflicted with a terminal illness.

It should be noted that this statement does not use the term "passive euthanasia." Instead, it speaks of "conservative passive medical care." Here is a reminder that the medical profession is hesitant to use the term "euthanasia," partly because the use of such distinctions as "passive" and "active" euthanasia has tended to blur the ethical dimensions inherent in the possibilities of extending and ending life almost at will. In normal medical parlance the term "euthanasia" stands for "mercy killing." As such this practice plays no rightful role in the profession of healing, and it has no place in the church except for purposes of condemnation.

To confound the whole field of definitions still more, the term "euthanasia" is sometimes modified by such adjectives as "voluntary," "involuntary" and "compulsory. " If euthanasia is voluntarily administered by and to oneself, it is a form of suicide. If applied by another with the deceased's consent or cooperation, it is both suicide and murder. If the application of a death-accelerating measure is administered by someone else without the consent of the patient or his family, it is called involuntary. If administered in violation of the wishes of the patient and/or the family, it is known as compulsory euthanasia. In an involuntary and/or a compulsory situation it is a form of murder. It is a patient-killer, not a pain-killer. In any form, it is illegal at the present time in every state.

The various semantic distinctions which have been indicated here, especially the use of "passive" or "active" and "positive" or "negative," serve to confuse the unwary and to desensitize those who oppose the legalization of mercy killing disguised as "happy death." In some cases the differentiations made may be well-intentioned. Yet the use of various qualifiers in connection with the term "euthanasia" has created great confusion, thereby raising unnecessary hazards for persons committed to a God-pleasing attitude regarding the issues of life and death.

Properly speaking euthanasia entails direct intervention, the killing of a human being, with or without his knowledge or consent. It may be briefly defined as the administration of a lethal dose to the patient or the deliberate refusal to use even the ordinary means of sustaining life. It is in this "active" sense that the word "euthanasia" will be used in the present study.

In discussing the legal status of euthanasia, the Report states that only in Uruguay are there legal provisions and regulations which permit magistrates to forego punishment where homicide is committed "out of compassion and at the victim's repeated request." In Switzerland and Germany, mitigation of punishment is permissible "where the killing proceeds from 'honorable motives.'" "The legality of acts of omission as a means of hastening death, or removing obstacles to its accomplishment, are still clouded with ambiguities" throughout the world. This second of the report concludes:

> While the foregoing discussion characterizes the current legal climate with respect to euthanasia and the identification of some of the principal arguments adduced by proponents of change, our own position as Lu-

theran Christians who seek to bring our conduct into conformity with
the divine will cannot, in the last analysis, be settled by purely secular
sanctions or from considerations of public policy alone. It is appropriate
at this time to include a reminder that resort to euthanasia would be
sinful even if the time should come when mercy killing may no longer
be defined by society as a crime.

Following a discussion of the meaning and significance of "life
and death" in which specific medical problems (Start Birth, Spina
Bifida, Advanced Malignancy, Brain Damage) are defined and attention is given to the significance of "ordinary and extraordinary
Means," the Report turns to "Ethics in Theological Focus." Life
"is the Creator's Gift" and "God created human beings to live and
not to die. Death in any form is inimical to what God originally
had in mind for His creation. Death is the last great enemy to be
overcome by the power of the risen Lord (1 Cor. 15:26). To speak
of 'death with dignity' or 'merciful release' therefore consists of
engaging in unholy rhetoric." The first section concludes with the
pronouncement:

> It is within God's purview alone to decide on the moment when the
> individual is to share that life which lies beyond death in a world restored
> to a splendor even greater than its pristine purity. Within the context
> of this certain hope, mercy killing runs squarely against the grain of
> the will of a gracious Creator . . .

Other issues considered under the heading of "Ethics" include "Life
and Death in View of Redemption" and "Life and Death in the
Light of Sanctification." Here, among other topics, the role of medical practitioners and the responsibility of the Christian community
are discussed.

The Report provides a recapitulation which concludes:

> While illness and death comprise an intrusion into life, they are
> allowed to carry on their destructive work under God's permissive will
> as reminders that we have here no abiding status and ought to look
> forward to the "city which has foundations, whose builder and maker
> is God" (Heb. 11:10). At the same time, pain and dying are experiences
> which can serve the further useful purpose of recalling people to the

awareness that they are not autonomous. Life as a gift from God is an endowment whose disposition lies in the hands of God Himself, working as Creator, Preserver, Savior and Sanctifier.

Against this background the suggestion of deliberately accelerating death runs counter to what the biblical revelation offers by way of both moral principle and spiritual insight into man's nature and destiny as these are woven into the fabric of God's saving intent. This situation calls for increased acceptance of the disciplinary challenges inherent in personal suffering as well as of the opportunities for service to the ill and the dying. Concurrently, the potentials of medical technology in all of its ramifications for good or ill make it imperative for the medical profession to rethink the whole matter of life and death in such a way as to do justice to the will of Him who created life in the first place and who has redeemed it and still keeps sanctifying it.

The Report closes with twelve "Guiding Principles" designed "to help individual Christians and groups of the faithful in their response to the issues which confront us in this area." The list includes the following:

1. Euthanasia, in its proper sense, is a synonym for mercy-killing, which involves suicide and/or murder. It is, therefore, contrary to God's law.
2. As Creator, God alone knows with certainty whether a disease or an injury is incurable.
3. When the God-given powers of the body to sustain its own life can no longer function and doctors in their professional judgment conclude that there is no real hope for recovery even with life-support instruments, a Christian may in good conscience "let nature take its course." Guidelines suggest that the patient (if capable of discussing the facts) be involved together with the doctor, the nearest of kin and the pastor.

In July, 1977, a special Task Force on Ethical Issues in Human Medicine in the Office of Research and Analysis of the American Lutheran Church published the results of a two-year study titled "Health, Life and Death . . . A Christian Perspective." In the foreword to the booklet, Carl F. Reuss, the Project Director, stated that the purpose of the booklet was "to stimulate thinking, promote discussion and motivate informed Christian response on issues of health, life, and death as seen in Christian perspectives." He warned that "Publication does not, however, constitute a declaration that the views expressed are the official policy and practice of The American Lutheran Church." Indeed, in the outlining of "Theological Understandings," the Task Force commented:

> Decision-making for Christians will imply both making approximate judgments about the quality of life, and relying on the mercy of God for guidance and forgiveness. The ambiguity of all human judgments is not sufficient reason for refusing to be specific as to what counts as "the quality of life." Just as we make human judgments about what counts as dangerous behavior by evil doers who must be restrained, and about what counts as innocent behavior by those who deserve to be protected, we can also make approximate judgments about what counts as that quality of life for which we strive on earth. (*Evangelical ethic*)

Sections E-12, 13, and 14 of the report discuss euthanasia. The removal of life-support systems is approved under certain humanitarian conditions, but active euthanasia is outlawed:

12. We affirm that in many instances heroic and extraordinary means used to prolong suffering of both the dying person and the loved ones is unkind. Wherever personality and personhood are permanently lost, artificial supportive measures often are seen as unfair to the dignity of the person and an extreme cost that is burdensome to the family. Families in these cases need not feel a burden of guilt for refusal to try unusual, heroic, and extraordinary life support. Where physicians have determined the irreversible phase of a terminal illness, we affirm that the person, young or old, has a right to peaceful death. As life draws to an end, with no hope for health restoration, permitting death is often the most heroic, caring, and charitable rendering of stewardship.

13. We affirm that every situation, in the context of dying persons, deserves consideration and decision on its own merit. We affirm that life is to be respected. Respect for the patient requires acceptance by others of that person's desires for life and death. Wise counsel by physicians, the clergy, and members of the health care

team should be made available to every family and person facing the crisis of death. Wherever possible, the dying person has a right to be informed of the nature of the illness and the likelihood of imminent death. One should be so informed in love.

14. We affirm that direct intervention to aid the irremediably deteriorating and hopelessly ill person to a swifter death is wrong. While direct intervention in many cases may appear "humane," deliberate injection of drugs or other means of terminating life are acts of intentional homicide. This deliberate act is far removed from decisions which allow people to die—like shutting off a life-supporting machine or even withholding medication. Permission for the normal process of death is an act of omission in the spirit of kindness and love within limits of Christian charity and legal concerns. Direct intervention to cause death, known as direct euthanasia, can not be permitted. We affirm there is a distinct moral difference between killing and allowing to die.

In response to the questionnaire, Dr. Edward D. Schneider, Assistant to the Presiding Bishop of the American Lutheran Church, indicated that the Church does believe in afterlife and divine judgment. Concerning the effect of active euthanasia on the afterlife of a participant in the act, Dr. Schneider wrote: "We believe it is an action contrary to the will of God, and therefore in need of forgiveness. We do not presume upon God's grace, but neither do we pronounce judgment which belongs to God." So far as the effects active euthanasia might have on funeral and burial rituals, Dr. Schneider noted that "This would depend upon the judgment of the pastor involved."

At the Eleventh Biennial Convention of the Lutheran Church in America, held in Louisville, Kentucky, Sept. 3–10, 1982, a statement on "Death and Dying" was formally adopted and later published in pamphlet form. In discussing the "Theological Perspectives on Death and Dying," various attitudes to death were presented, including death as "natural" (Gen. 25:8), as "tragic" (Psalm 6:4), as "friend" and as "enemy" (I Corinthians 15:56). The Christian concept of "Victory Over Death" (Romans 6:4, 8:38–39) concluded the section. The comments on "Ethical Decision-Making" made the familiar reference to life as a gift from God and called for respect for the integrity of the life process, which includes both birth and death, and for both living and dying occurring within "a caring community." The individual's rights in determining treatment, a call for "truthfulness and faithfulness" in human relations, and the significance of "hope and meaning in life" were all stressed.

If a patient is irreversibly dying with a progressive disease for which no effective therapy exists, "As the final stages of the dying process occur, there comes a time to recognize the reality of what is happening by refraining from attempts to resuscitate the person and by discontinuing the use of artificial life-support systems. To try desperately to maintain the vital signs of an irreversibly dying person for whom death is imminent is inconsistent with a Christian ethic that mandates respect for dying, as well as for living." On the other hand, any involvement in active euthanasia is absolutely forbidden:

> Deliberately administering a lethal drug in order to kill the patient, or otherwise taking steps to cause death, is quite a different matter. This is frequently called "active euthanasia" or "mercy killing" (as contrasted with the cases discussed above, which involve withholding or withdrawing medical treatment, thereby allowing death to occur from a disease or injury).
>
> Some might maintain that active euthanasia can represent an appropriate course of action if motivated by the desire to end suffering. Christian stewardship of life, however, mandates treasuring and preserving the life which God has given, be it our own life or the life of some other person. This view is supported by the affirmation that meaning and hope are possible in all of life's situations, even those involving great suffering. To depart from this view by performing active euthanasia, thereby deliberately destroying life created in the image of God, is contrary to Christian conscience.
>
> Whatever the circumstances, it must be remembered that the Christian commitment to caring community mandates reaching out to those in distress and sharing hope and meaning in life which might elicit a renewed commitment to living.

Some understanding of the kind of wrestling with issues that lie behind reports of this nature may be inferred, in part, from articles published by ethicists and theologians. For example, James M. Childs, Jr., who teaches theology and ethics at Concordia Senior College,

Fort Wayne, Indiana, touched on basic questions in his essay, "Euthanasia: An Introduction to a Moral Dilemma," which appeared in *Currents in Theology and Mission* (pp. 67–78). Prof. Childs notes that euthanasia is "a borderline situation in which every right and wrong is not evident in every case and most cases fall within the gray area of decision-making. The borderline situation arises as a result of the 'fallenness' of our world in which normal moral laws are confounded by the world's abnormal condition."

For instance, as he discusses indirect euthanasia, he notes that "the use of painkillers that relieve the suffering of the terminal patient . . . may also contribute to hastening his death." He does not challenge the intentions of those who favor indirect euthanasia and he comments: "Behind the judgment of all those who approve indirect euthanasia is the recognition that the prolongation of life without any hope of recovery soon becomes tantamount to violence against life by prolonging the agonies of death." But the problem does not end here:

> Nonetheless, acceptance of indirect euthanasia in principle does not make decision easy. It has been common to seek help in deciding by making the distinction between ordinary and extraordinary means of treatment. We are normally not obligated to use extraordinary measures that promise no significant results. What is ordinary in one case may be extraordinary in another when it cannot contribute to a cure. Things as commonplace as intravenous feeding, oxygen tents and antibiotics can become extraordinary if the situation is so severe as to indicate that they prolong life unnecessarily and that the patient is not even aware of them as an expression of comfort and care. Making such a determination is easier to talk about than it is to do. Withdrawal of oxygen, shutting off a respirator or disconnecting the intravenous tubes are simple, straightforward acts of denying a human being the basic elements of life: air, food, and water. It is at this point that we sense how close the act of omission comes to acts of commission.

Following a discussion of the ways in which various theologians and ethicists have confronted these problems, Childs raises the question "Who Decides?" Here he lists some qualifications for decision making:

First of all, as Christians we do not believe that our lives are ours to dispense with as we choose. God is the creator, preserver and redeemer of our lives. Christian conscience cannot countenance any means of euthanasia that is an act of unfaith which despairs of the Lord's help in time of suffering. At the same time, desperate attempts to cling to life at all costs may also reflect a lack of trust in the promise of life everlasting in Christ. Secondly, a patient is surely dependent upon the expertise and counsel of his doctors and his decision will be shaped by the information they give. Thirdly, the right of the patient to decide is limited by the rights of others attending him. He cannot expect medical personnel and family to act against conscience, even though he has a legal right to refuse treatment and may even secure a court order to that effect. Fourthly, the patient's right to decide is further bounded by his own condition. When extreme pain and suffering set in, one's capacity to understand and direct one's own situation is greatly affected. Finally, a patient is bound by the law as it impinges on his estate should his act be judged a suicide, and as it impinges on medical staff who may be subject to prosecution for aiding and abetting a suicide or even for homicide.

If a patient is comatose, the decision is to be made by the medical staff, the family, and the clergy. Childs recognizes the assistance that a Living Will provides in such a situation. He believes that "The primary concern of Christian ethics is not whether one can justify life-taking under certain conditions, but how one can best act on the positive obligations to love and care for the other person. This is the fundamental thrust of *agape*-love." Because Christians recognize that humans are created in "the image of God for immediate, personal communion and union with their creator," they know that a command implicit in creation and "elsewhere made explicit . . . requires that we do not take life, that we do no harm, that we seek to preserve life, and that we seek to ameliorate all suffering, pain, and disease that is destructive of personal humanity." How does one interpret this belief in terms of the issue of euthanasia?

If, for example, we are considering the possibility of indirect euthanasia in an apparently hopeless case, we need to interpret how our positive obligations toward human life are applicable to the withdrawal of extraordinary means or even of all means of life support. If our conclusion is that no method we possess can reverse the dying, then the obligation to preserve life ceases to be relevant and gives way to another dimension of our respect and love for lives: the relief of suffering and the opposition to all things which dehumanize and denigrate humanity. Our care for the dying demands that we avoid the sort of medical heroics that will finally become an aggression against life by prolonging the person's dying rather than preserving meaningful personal existence for even a short time. At the same time, the decision to withdraw or withhold certain measures for patients who are even slightly able to sense the presence of our care should not include withdrawing measures that are comforting and that enhance our ability to communicate that care.

Childs cautioned against being too ready to make decisions in such circumstances:

We need to fight the almost ingrained conviction that if persons cannot care for themselves and be productive in a normal way, they are not fully human, cannot have a meaningful life, and have a questionable right to live. When the dying and the defective reach that conclusion about themselves, it is up to those who care to prove them wrong.

Insofar as active or direct euthanasia is concerned, Childs' position is that of the Lutheran Church. He argues that, first of all, it is wrong in principle in that it is contrary "to a generally formulated absolute which forbids life-taking and commits us to the preservation of life." He does recognize that conflicts of "absolutes" may occur and that feelings of guilt can be developed. His second objection introduces the 'domino' or 'wedge' theories, which imply that excesses may result if "direct euthanasia were to be permitted in principle." He recalls the Nazi experience and quotes a Florida physician-legislator who suggested that the state could save five billion dollars over the next fifty years if all the mongoloids were allowed to succumb to the pneumonia they frequently contract.

His third objection is that "only God can make an end to life." But, he comments: "To the extent that it means we can abdicate struggling with responsible decision-making in the care of the dying,

I think it is wrong." He recognizes that to rest a case solely on the divine "lordship of life" could mean the refraining from certain life-saving measures. He summarizes his general approach as follows:

> When death is inevitable and meaningful life is not present, an obligation to relieve suffering takes over and we may need to cooperate with the patient's dying. This involves withdrawal of "extraordinary" life-support measures and/or the administration of pain-relievers that may shorten life. This course of action may obtain when a child is born for whom only artificial life support can enable survival and for whom there is no hope of life apart from this. It may also obtain in cases of brain death and/or irreversible loss of consciousness where there can be no hope for the recovery of spontaneous vital function. Finally, it may obtain in a case of a person facing irreversible dying in unrelieved agony.

The moral dilemma of such situations compels Childs to comment that ". . . the extreme situation of conflict that forces us to compromise one absolute demand in favor of another, whether we choose euthanasia or not, is a compromise of tragic dimensions with which we have to contend."

The Reformed Tradition

The World Alliance of Reformed Churches appears to have taken no stand on euthanasia. The Rev. James E. Andrews, Stated Clerk of the Presbyterian Church (USA), in response to question #1 of the questionnaire, suggests, that in his opinion: "The organization would be opposed to the artificial prolongation of life in hopeless situations."

With respect to my survey question #2, Mr. Andrews was unable to provide any estimates of response except to suggest that in the second and third portions of the question the percentages of approving votes would drop appreciably.

He states, with respect to #3:

The confessional positions of the member Churches of the World Alliance of Reformed Churches unanimously support the concept of life after human death. The development of thought about medical ethics has not progressed to the point of evaluating participation in active euthanasia with regard to its impact upon the spiritual state (salvation) of the patient or one who participated in the termination of the patient's life. These would be dealt with in traditional terms such as suicide, and homicide.

It is not in the tradition of the Reformed Churches "to extol the deceased nor to estimate the deceased's spiritual state at death." Funeral services emphasize confidence in the love of God through

Jesus Christ. Nor does the World Alliance "participate in the establishment of standards" for counseling in the situations set forth in questions five and six.

The Rev. Thomas McElhinney, a pastor in the Presbyterian Church (USA), made reference in his response to the statement adopted by the 1983 General Assembly of the Presbyterian Church (USA) entitled "The Covenant of Life and the Caring Community." (This statement is discussed below.) Dr. McElhinney indicated that the answer to the first question in the questionnaire would be "yes" and that although the response to question #2 would be divided, "most would understand it." Most would tend to condemn assisted suicide, but a sizeable minority would accept it. Except for very conservative members, most would agree that the participation in active suicide would have no affect on the afterlife.

Back of the statement "The Covenant of Life and the Caring Community," which was published in *Church and Society* (July/August 1983), was a working committee which prefaced its presentation of the policy statement with material reflecting its research into biblical, theological and ethical issues. The background study covered such items as "Where Are We Coming From?" and considered "The Church as a Covenant People," which presented the biblical foundation for statements about the dignity of human life and the church as a caring community. Another topic included was "Where Are We in the Development of Biomedical Technology?" But the section dealing with "Decision Making at the End of Life," which was published in *Church and Society* and which is reproduced below, is the most significant for the purposes of our inquiry.

In the pre-statement study, it was stated:

The biomedical implications of the theology of death and eternal life reflected in contemporary theologians are several. (1) We fight with God against the power of death; (2) We hope for a time in history when disease and untimely death will be overcome; (3) We accept death as a part of life experience; (4) We do not live under the dominion of death but live toward the promise of life; (5) We trust the details to God; and (6) In life and death we are with God.

Following this statement, the study turned to "The Ethics of Life and Death." Seven important points were made:

1. The direction of Biblical ethics is against taking the life of another even for benevolent reasons. Persons should not be deemed worthless, too old, too weak, unproductive, sociopathic or a burden, thereby justifying some act of positive "mercy killing," or the more fashionable slow killing by neglect. When persons fall into deep sickness, pain, suffering, unconsciousness; when they lie helpless under deep sedation or at the brink of danger in intensive care, they must know that they will not be abandoned.

   While the direction of Biblical ethics is against taking the life of another, it in no way claims that it is necessary to prolong the life— or the dying process—of a person who is gravely ill with little or no hope for cure or remission. Persons who are terminally ill must be able to trust that their dying will not be prolonged by unrequested technological interventions. As theologian Paul Ramsey has stated, "We need . . . to discover the moral limits properly surrounding efforts to save life. We need to recover the meaning of only caring for the dying, and the justification—indeed the obligation—of intervening against many a medical intervention that is possible today." The existence of specific medical technology does not require that it be used. . . .

2. Most discussion of ethics in health care addresses the issue of autonomy (i.e., a person's right to make—or at least participate in— decisions related to his/her own body), primarily when discussing death and dying. The popular cliches related to this issue are: "the right to die," "death with dignity" and the "right to refuse treatment." Although cases (Quinlan, Fox, Saikewicz) which have been prominent in the mass news media and which have focused on these extraordinary issues are more dramatic than commonplace, they still necessitate a moral response. *In a pluralistic society where people have different beliefs about life and death, basic Christian respect for persons demands that a person's decisions about death be honored in most instances.* (Emphasis mine: G.A.L.)

   The choice of whether or not to undergo further treatment, whether or not to consent to experimental therapy, or to donate tissue should be a personal decision. Since the atmosphere of critical care medicine is highly charged with values such as medical authority, vested interest and patient submission, care should be taken by the physician to converse freely and candidly with the patient. The patient ought to know the options, the pros and cons of each option, the thoughts of the attending clinicians, and then be encouraged to make their own decision. Two extremes must be avoided. The first extreme position paternalistically decides for patients what is best and then announces that decision. This view holds that it is unkind or unreasonable to invite the patient into the debate over options (and that the physician knows best) and so proceeds to make proxy decisions for the patient. The second unfortunate course sets the options and scenarios before the patient like a computer. It gives the probabilities and statistics and then says, "There you are, now decide!" Both of these approaches shrink from the pain and reward of cooperative judgment. The best course is one which involves coming to a thoughtful medical judgment, sharing this with the patient, reviewing the alternative courses, and inviting the patient's response. The tragedy of patient refusal—or thoughtless acceptance—of procedures and the increased possibility of legal action often arise from failure to respect the patient's humanity and enter into reponsible dialogue with them.

Another variation on paternalistic decision making involves the externally imposed judgment about patient's quality of life. If a patient's quality of life is deemed unsuitable or intolerable by members of the health care team, treatment may be terminated—or not initiated—and the patient allowed to die. This judgment about a person's quality of life made by someone other than the patient is far different from an individual's making such a decision about their own life quality. While members of the health care professions are called upon to make quality of life decisions at many levels—and it is unrealistic to deny that such decisions are not necessary—a word of caution is in order to those who make such decisions and to all who may be patients at some point in time. We must take great care not to denigrate the worth or life of others and impose a judgement of poor quality, which might provide justification for stopping treatment or avoiding the patient. . . .

3. The real, almost inevitable danger of reducing human lives to statistic or mechanical processes must be acknowledged. The influences of economic factors often unspoken, loom large. The efforts to place economic values on patients' lives or determine how many treatments an individual deserves. While reprehensible, nonetheless they occur. If medical care must be rationed (e.g., dialysis after 60 years of age),

policies should be made following public deliberation so that those affected will have had a chance to participate. . . .

4. There is a danger and temptation to idolize bodily life by making retention of physical life the only good and primary goal. Jesus touches the subject when he says that "Whoever would save his life shall lose it." Too much effort to defend one's own life, to bury it in a safe place like the one talent man, to refuse to give life away, or to fail to use it up goes against the grain of Christian calling. It is indeed idolatrous to try to keep a person's body alive no matter how empty that life may be. Human beings are transcendent creatures. Real life comes from beyond bodily function. Jesus asks: "Is not life more than food and the body than clothing?" (Matthew 6:25b). Often hospitals and medical personnel are simply engaged in a contest to preserve "life", with little concern for quality or expectation. Sometimes they win the battle, but the patient loses. Clinging to life rather than reaching out to life compounds the tragedy.

5. The affirmation about eternal life that is woven into the Gospel according to John should be emphasized. Eternal life is here and now. According to the Apostle Paul, the light of promise shines in the present moment. Eternal life, not death, is the ultimate reality. That assurance keeps Christians from living all of life being afraid of death. For Christians the adventure is never toward an end but toward new beginnings. Elizabeth Kubler-Ross has written that death is the final stage of growth; it would be more appropriate to affirm that death is another stage of becoming. For Christians, death can be understood as the next chapter in the surprising story of life.

6. Decision making is never sure; deciders are seldom secure. Persons are ambivalent about whether to approach death with dread or hope, whether to resist or to accept. Possibly this ambivalence comes from the built-in will to live and the corresponding will to die. Whatever its origin, ambivalence is woven into the fabric of being itself, and decisions of life and death are met with a kind of frustrating ambiguity. Since life-death decisions can rarely be made with certainty, even when all the evidence is in, decisions must be made with humility and with a posture of seeking God's forgiveness and acceptance.

7. Finally, the Church is in the world to be an example, not to impose value or beliefs. By its life and its attitude toward life, it can and should bear witness to the faith. The Church in this area, as in many others, must be the community of care, protection and nurture. In

this way, the Church can be a model in a pluralistic society for how these decisions ought to be made while preserving and enhancing human dignity and worth.

The preliminary study included as appendices a Living Will, a set of guidelines titled "Directions for My Care, A Christian Affirmation of Life," and a "Form or Declaration Under the Voluntary Euthanasia Act of 1969." The "Directions for My Care" document states:

> If my death is near and cannot be avoided, and if I have lost the ability to interact with others and have no reasonable chance of regaining this ability, or if my suffering is intense and irreversible, I do not want to have my life prolonged. I would then ask not to be subjected to surgery or resuscitation. Nor would I then wish to have life support from mechanical ventilators, intensive care services, or other life prolonging procedures, including the administration of antibiotics and blood products . . .

The Directions provided for the appointment of a person authorized to act on the patient's behalf.

The Christian Affirmation is addressed to family, friends, physician, lawyer, and clergyman. The first half is a statement of belief in God as creator and sustainer of life, a belief in Jesus Christ as the prefigurer of resurrection who makes possible the anticipated death-resurrection process, and a belief in the worth and dignity of each individual in the conviction that God "has entrusted to me a shared dominion with him over my earthly existence so that I am bound to use ordinary means to preserve my life but I am free to refuse extraordinary means to prolong my life," and in the acceptance of death as "a free human act which enables me to surrender this life and to be united with God for eternity."

The second part of the Affirmation requests that the individual be informed of approaching death in order to prepare for it. It is important that the patient be consulted about all medical treatment, that unbearable pain be alleviated, but that "no means should be used with the intention of shortening my life." Further, the dying person is joined by friends, family, and the whole Christian community "in prayer and mortification as I prepare for the great personal act of dying."

The Declaration Under the Voluntary Euthanasia Act has three parts:

1. If I should at any time suffer from a serious physical illness or impairment reasonably thought in my case to be incurable and expected to cause me severe distress or render me incapable of rational existence, I request the administration of euthanasia at a time or in circumstances to be indicated or specified by me or, if it is apparent that I have become incapable of giving directions, at the discretion of the physician in charge of my case.

2. In the event of my suffering from any of the conditions specified above, I request that no active steps should be taken, and in particular that no resuscitatory techniques should be used, to prolong my life or restore me to consciousness.

3. This declaration is to remain in force unless I revoke it, which I may do at any time, and any request I may make concerning action to be taken or withheld in connection with this declaration will be made without further formalities.

    I wish it to be understood that I have confidence in the good faith of my relatives and physicians, and fear degeneration and indignity far more than I fear premature death. I ask and authorize the physician in charge of my case to bear these statements in mind when considering what my wishes would be in any uncertain situation.

Some details of the study have been presented here because of the sensitivity to differing points of view and the willingness to accept the pluralistic nature of the human community. There appears to be no desire to press the findings or attitudes of the Presbyterian Church USA on any other group. Furthermore, the study carefully examines existing policies and attitudes in the medical and religious communities and provides guidelines for the protection of human rights and the recognition that the desires of individuals may differ. Finally, the study makes an effort to deal with the legal dimensions confronting individuals who wish to have a voice in determining how their final days will be spent. It is my feeling that much of what is reprinted here can serve as an example for other religious communities.

The conclusion of the policy statement adopted by the 195th General Assembly of the Presbyterian Church USA and published in *Church and Society,* 1983, was titled "Decision Making at the End of Life." It read as follows:

1. Many members of the Presbyterian Church will face health care decisions toward the end of life which they could not have anticipated and many of those decisions will require judgments that relate to values held by the patient. Therefore, the 195th General Assembly (1983) calls upon its members to:

   a. Select their physicians with regard not only to the skillfulness of the medical care which they can provide, but for their values regarding human life and community, whenever such a choice is available.
   b. Take time to reflect on their own values and discuss these with family members, close friends, and their clergy.
   c. Speak with their physicians about their concerns regarding care and become educated about their condition in order to permit informed decision making.
   d. Provide instructions (and designate two agents to carry our instruction) with regard to extraordinary therapies and treatments to prolong life.

2. The church should be a place where individuals and families can make plans about death, manner of death, living wills, etc. Therefore, the 195th General Assembly (1983) calls upon the church:

   a. To request the program agencies to make available information and study tools for use by congregations, regarding options available at the end of life and means of informing health care professionals of their wishes.
   b. To hold seminars utilizing the aforementioned materials and/or qualified resource persons whenever possible.
   c. To advocate that human need and benevolence replace the opportunism and exploitation that so often surround the death experience presently.

3. Harmony and integration should be sought between intensive care, curative hospitals, and hospices so that end-of-life care can be free from jurisdictional conflict and therapeutic and palliative care are available to all.

Individual pastors of the Church of Scotland have also called for use of the Living Will and for passive euthanasia. The Rev. Ean Simpson, minister of Kerse Church, Grangemouth, Stirlingshire, in an address to the General Assembly of the Church of Scotland in 1978, called for respect for differing attitudes toward euthanasia. His comments were published in the summer 1980 edition of "The Newsletter of Exit":

Now I well realize that there are patients and doctors who are opposed to euthanasia on principle, and I respect their stand. By the same token, therefore, those of us who are involved, whether as a doctor or a minister, in helping terminally ill people to die peacefully and with dignity have the right to receive similar respect for our wishes. I believe that no person or group of persons, however well-intentioned, should have the right to dictate terms of dying to the incurably ill. If anyone believes on conscience sake that he should die without the merciful help of drugs, then he must be free to do so. But it is quite wrong to demand that others who do not share his belief follow the same course.

Mr. Simpson took issue with the argument that "it is the Christian duty to face maximum pain" and said that he would like to take some of those who propose this idea "to some bedsides where both relatives and staff are nearly driven frantic by the pleas for release from severely ill patients." He added: "To argue that it is the Christian duty to conquer pain is fine when the loved one is going into a gentle, peaceful decline. But the suggestion becomes a mockery of empty words when you are confronted with a man or woman literally screaming for death." He protested that his statements were "not purely an emotional reaction on my part," but were related to the "harsh facts surrounding terminal illness in many cases. Doctors and nurses are helpless and the minister is merely the impotent symbol of a belief that suffering here will be rewarded with glory there. "Dying well" sounds splendidly admirable in the committee-room, but it has no place in the face of the realities of the hospital ward." The Rev. Mr. Simpson concluded with an appeal for the use of the Living Will. According to Sheila Little, Chairman of The Voluntary Euthanasia Society of Scotland, Mr. Simpson addressed the General Assembly again in 1980, but apparently his appeal went unheeded and he received no general support for his position.

The Rev. Gavin McCallum, who is a member of Scottish Exit, wrote a brief article in the Spring 1981 edition of that organization's newsletter. He pointed out that "Christ by his teachings and miracles showed that suffering was against God's will and that man must cooperate with God to relieve it." Further, he anticipated that "A time will come for everyone when the body should be allowed to die with dignity, freeing relatives and friends from strain, setting the soul free from an aching body or a sick mind, and allowing the individual to enter into the peace of his Father's House."

Writing in the Summer, 1981, issue of the newsletter of Scottish Exit, the Rev. Alistair Bennett, a retired minister of the Church of Scotland, commented on the use of the Bible as a guide for the ethics of euthanasia:

There is a gulf of over twenty centuries between then and now, between them and us. The Bible speaks of great moral and spiritual truths but the evaluation of these truths and their implication and application today will be very different from what it was so very long ago. They could not forsee our situation and we can never go back to theirs. Like them we must have the courage to form our own judgements and intimate our own behaviour, responding to the situation in which we live. The difference will be that we will make our judgements enlightened by modern knowledge and empowered by modern technology and threatened by modern population. We would be moral cowards and unworthy descendants if we tried to lean back and expect our ancestors to make our decisions.

In Biblical times, both Old and New Testament, people firmly believed that illness was caused by evil spirits or was a sign of the punishment of God. Like all his contemporaries Jesus shared the same belief. People had little understanding of the constitution or working of the human body and no knowledge whatever of bacterial or viral infection.

Birth, illness, age and death were all shadowed by ignorance and superstition and fear. For us the whole situation has been transformed. The birth and growth of medical knowledge and its prodigious advances in this century have brought astonishing new comprehensions and armed us with sweeping new powers which can be blessedly benign or catastrophically malevolent, according as we use them. It is within this age of change and innovation that we have been born and within it we are fated to live and to die. We cannot turn back the clock. We must adapt to our environment. This is the human adventure.

But Mr. Bennett is sensitive to the deep spiritual concerns of the Christian community:

There is one question which is bound to lurk at the back of the mind of those who have been brought up under orthodox Christian teaching. What if there is a life to come? Would anyone who contributed to their own death here be punished there? The uncertain vision of a life to come, which has so many versions, should never divert us from dealing realistically with the actual problems of this present life. Evidence for another life is hard to find, while evidence for the needs of this life moves urgently in our bodies every day. The distant dream does not cancel out the dull pain. Will there be punishment? It is a hypothetical question. No one on earth has the answer.

The Methodist Church

At the last full meeting of the World Methodist Council, although the Council "expressed its mind on a number of issues and concerns, euthanasia was not one of them," according to Joe Hale, a representative. However, at a meeting of the General Council of the United Methodist Church in Portland, Oregon, in May 1976, a statement relating social principles was issued. The portion on euthanasia, passed without debate, read: "We assert the right of every person to die in dignity with loving personal care and without efforts to prolong terminal illnesses merely because the technology is available to do so."

In 1980, the General Council adopted the following statement on "Death With Dignity":

> We applaud medical science for efforts to prevent disease and illness and for advances in treatment that extend the meaningful life of human beings. At the same time, in the varying stages of death and life that advances in medical science have occasioned, we recognize the agonizing personal and moral decisions faced by the dying, their physicians, their families, and their friends. Therefore, we assert the right of every person to die in dignity, with loving personal care and without efforts to prolong terminal illnesses merely because the technology is available to do so.

Neither statement addresses the issues of euthanasia directly, but acceptance of passive euthanasia seems to be clearly implied. Haviland C. Housten, General Secretary of the General Board of Church and Society of the United Methodist Church, indicates that the 1980 statement "incorporates all we have in terms of position statements on the issue of euthanasia."

Claiming no authority "beyond that of a 'good Methodist,'" the Rev. the Lord Soper, former President of the Methodist Conference and a recipient of the Methodist World Conference Prize for Peace, addressed the International Conference on Euthanasia and Suicide at Oxford, in September, 1980. He stressed his belief that "the Christian faith is a developing, and not a static thing," and enunciated "the fundamental principles within which I find myself in fervent support of the principles of voluntary euthanasia . . . Christianity begins in a sacramental view of life."

> When we come to human beings it may surprise some people when I make this the cardinal point: that the sacramental view of life demands that we see human beings in an eternal concept and not in a temporal one. It strikes me as somewhat ludicrous that people who profess their ardent desire to get to heaven use the most scrupulous precautions to keep themselves here on earth.
>
> The fact that lies beyond any doubt is that the way we think of a Christian view of voluntary euthanasia must depend ultimately on what we regard as the sacramental view of man. That's where Christianity starts. Now what is the nature of this Christian faith? It is the law of love. The Christian's love is compounded of active compassion. Any expression of the law, as of course dear old Saint Paul knew, must ultimately be set within the general framework of love.

Lord Soper continued and explicated his beliefs concerning the "relevance" of voluntary euthanasia:

> . . . to remove the fear of dying, not the fear of death, but the fear of all the terrible and nauseating conditions that very often prevail. And when death is coming, not to be kept from that other world in which many a Christian—in fact all Christians—should believe.
>
> This to me is common sense, the common sense that proceeds from the belief above everything else that love is the fulfillment of the law, and must take precedence over every category of law.
>
> The one thing that above everything else I have been taught over the years is that it is idle to talk in terms of sacredness and of love and of

compassion until you're prepared to try, however imperfectly, to carry them out within the framework of everyday society.

What we have to do, surely, is to express this within the kind of framework which will exercise an effect in its turn upon those who, at the moment, are largely blinded by prejudice.

If you ask me what is the Christian view with regard to euthanasia I can, without any doubt, recommend it in the terms of my own father who, at the end of his life—and it was a very full and in many ways a saintly life—complained somewhat bitterly to me that the doctors were hindering his approach to the celestial world to which he had looked forward for the whole of his life. He wanted to go home. And—in the simplest terms—what right has any of us to prevent somebody who wants to go home from starting on that journey unhindered by all the drugs and stupidities that belong to a materialistic age?

This is an age in which we contrive to believe that the scientific concept of life is the final satisfactory one. It is nothing of the sort.

Jesus said 'Seek ye first the Kingdom of God and its righteousness, and all things necessary will be added to that discovery '.

In the voluntary euthanasia effort I find one expression of a loving and sacramental concept.

To be sure, Lord Soper's remarks reflect his own beliefs and cannot be taken as representative of the Methodist Church in Britain or elsewhere. As the heading of this address in the Autumn, 1981 issue of the Scottish Exit newsletter warns us, "Christian Views on Euthanasia Vary Enormously."

Bishop F. C. James of the African Methodist Church stated, "We do not sanction any form of death by other than natural or accidental causes." Although euthanasia is considered to be a violation of the commandment "Thou shalt not kill," burial rites would not be affected. The advice to anyone contemplating euthanasia would simply be, "Don't do it!"

The Mennonite Church

Key persons in the Mennonite Church provided answers to the questionnaire. Dr. David Ewart, who has been a member of the Board of Reference and Counsel—the Mennonites' spiritual overseers of faith and life—wrote in answer to my survey question #1: "If the person who is dying, in consultation with family and physician agree to end the suffering by removing the life-support system, I believe that would be acceptable. Whereas technology is a gift of God to man, it is abused when it is used to sustain life artificially." Vern Preheim of the General Conference Mennonite Church suggests that passive euthanasia would probably be accepted but "with mixed feelings." John K. Stoner, Executive Secretary of the Peace Section, wrote, "In brief, my understanding of the generally held Mennonite position would be that most Mennonite groups would sanction the removal of life-support systems in the case of patients similar to the one described in example #1. In other words, 'passive' euthanasia would be approved on the grounds that death is ultimately inevitable and is to be accepted."

Dr. Erland Waltner, Executive Secretary of the Mennonite Medical Association, wrote:

The Mennonite Medical Association, as a professional rather than an ecclesiastical organization, has taken no formal position on the issue of "passive euthanasia." "Positions" then would be taken in local congregations, by pastoral leaders, and more specifically by families con-

90

sulting with their pastor and their doctor. My own position, shared by numerous others, would be open to what is above called "passive euthanasia" on the grounds that death can be accepted as God's own way of releasing persons from physical suffering while certain "heroic measures" of life-support may be undue resistance to normal/natural completion of life, even at the age of 22.

With regard to question #2 and active euthanasia, Dr. Waltner wrote:

Again, no formal positions have been taken, but especially because Mennonites affirm that human life is a sacred trust from God and thus take a formal position against its destruction by active means, such as by war or by abortion, we would not approve participation in the hastening of the death process, though we accept death as a normal/ natural process in human experience. Neither suicide nor active participation in suicide of a suffering patient would find general approval, though many would express a high level of compassion for those suffering in the way described above and would have a measure of "understanding" without approving "active euthanasia."

Vern Preheim suggests that active euthanasia would probably not be acceptable because it "is seen as killing." Dr. Ewart commented:

It is one matter to remove the life-support system when a person is dying. It is another matter to inflict death or hurry it on. Suicide is viewed by us as a violation of the sacredness of life. Our denomination holds also that killing in war is contrary to the Scriptures, as is abortion. Active euthanasia would fall in the same category.

The effect of euthanasia on the afterlife "is not articulated in our beliefs," according to Dr. Waltner. He comments, "We understand the term 'soul' as used biblically to designate the SELF and not some 'fragment' of personhood. We do believe that the SELF has an afterlife and that Divine Judgment is a part of eternal reality. . . . Eternal salvation is seen as a gift of Divine Grace." Nick Rempel, Secretary of the Mennonite Brethren Church, wrote, "The Afterlife is not based upon do's or don'ts—not a meritorious gain

—but a gift of *grace* through faith in the person of Jesus Christ. Judgment belongs to God!"

The funeral rites would not be affected by euthanasia. "Once the person is dead," wrote Dr. Ewart, "one is concerned with the living who are left behind and not with the corpse." Similarly, Nick Rempel stated, "The funeral service would be in the Church—again, judgment belongs to God—we would not make a judgment about eternal destiny." Dr. Waltner does not believe that the fact of euthanasia would affect the ritual, but he qualifies his statement by pointing out that it may depend on the local pastor and/or congregation. The burial of one who has committed suicide is generally handled with deep sensitivity for the grief being endured by the survivors and respect for the 'unknown factors' in 'cause of death.'"

Nick Rempel states that in the matter of counseling for passive euthanasia, "If the quality of life is such that only heroic measures will prolong it—and if prolonging it has serious economic and emotional demands upon the family—we would probably counsel to take off the support system —allow death to come." Dr. Stoner wrote that, "Questions of the stewardship of limited funds and resources for the care of patients in extreme conditions would figure in. Many Mennonites would feel that it is unjust to spend thousands of dollars to prolong the life of a dying person for days or weeks when those dollars applied to basic health service for children in a needy country of the world could prevent brain damage and save lives." Dr. Waltner believes that the likely counsel would be "to continue to trust God. Prayer for 'release' (death) on the part of the patient and of the pastor may be appropriate."

Counseling for active euthanasia would tend to discourage such action. Dr. Waltner believes that "In this case, more support would be given to 'patient endurance' with allowance for prayer that God may bring suffering to completion." According to Vern Preheim, the scriptural basis for the Mennonite position is the commandment "Thou shalt not kill." David Ewart adds: "Our view of the sacredness of life is based on the Bible's teaching that God is the Creator and therefore also the Lord over life."

The Church of the Brethren

Ron Waters of the Brethren Church in Ashland, Ohio, wrote, "We have taken no official position, but we would generally be opposed to active euthanasia." Robert W. Neff, General Secretary of the General Brotherhood Board of the Church of the Brethren, provided a copy of a document titled "Life Stewardship," which was passed in June, 1975, at the Church of the Brethren Annual Conference—"the highest decision-making body in the Church." The statement began with comments on the "Biblical View of the Body":

> In the Creation account given to us in Genesis 2 we find that man is completely dependent upon the grace of God for his personal existence: *Then the Lord God formed man of dust from the ground, and breathed into his nostrils the breath of life; and man became a living being* (Gen. 2:7). Apart from the breath, or Spirit, of God, the human body is merely worthless dust.

The report goes on to note that in most of the Old Testament, there is no belief in any personal life beyond death, but that the New Testament proclaims there is a resurrection of the dead.

The next portions review "Historical Positions Regarding the Funeral and Burial," "The Christian Funeral, The Church as a Support Community," and "Christian Stewardship in Relation to Medical Need, the Funeral and Estate Planning." The importance of grief counseling is stressed, and the use of "heroic" medical measures is addressed from the point of view both of physicians and of laity.

The query implies concern for "heroic medical measures that merely maintain life, but deny the terminally ill the dignity of dying in peace." This is a problem in some instances, though seldom intentional. According to a recent survey, the vast majority of doctors recognize no special duty to keep terminally ill patients alive. (The 1974 Annual Conference survey shows that 55% of the delegates who participated in it did not feel that "the doctor should keep you alive as long as possible.") However, in large, research-oriented institutions, it is more likely that "everything possible" will be tried, with no member of the treatment team being willing to admit defeat, or to take responsibility for the new phase of treatment of the person. Moreover, the patient is isolated from his home, thus cultural and community strengths cannot be utilized at this very important time. The dying patient is reduced to a set of complaints, symptoms, and physical findings, and the question is seldom asked, *Did the patient die peacefully, with self-esteem, dignity, and in control of his limited options?*

The patient often finds himself fed, bathed, sent for tests, X-rayed, intubated, awakened, sedated, medicated—sometimes without any active participation in the decisions. The *patient*—not the doctor, family, church, or society—has the right to be considered in these decisions, and acknowledging this right contributes to his dignity and humanity.

The problem of "heroic medical measures" at the time of death is not purely a problem for the physicians, for far too many people believe that something more can be done for the fatally ill when in reality nothing can. The ever-widening expectance of treatments for cancer, heart, and kidney diseases, for example, make the acceptance of death more and more difficult, not only for the physician, who feels some sense of obligation to maintain treatment until the very end, but also for the families, who fear the ensuing guilt when "everything possible" isn't done. Even patients who probably suspect that they are dying, may not face the issue, but may fantasize potential breakthroughs for their particular disease.

There is justification for our concern about misapplication of "heroic medical measures." A few examples are truly horror stories of continued suffering, enormous expense, and the breakdown of the remaining family for the support of vegetative "life." Few, if any, are comfortable with this outcome, and many, through the signing of a "living will," hope to actively prevent such an occurrence. The Living Will is a signed and witnessed document which states that "at such time when there is no reasonable expectation of my recovering from physical or mental illness, I request that I not be kept alive by artificial means or heroic measures, and that I be allowed to die with dignity. " A growing movement now asserts that there is a right to die, as well as a right to live, and that the right to die is often violated by the prolonged, excruciating, and expensive medical interventions that keep people alive who would be better off dead.

Unfortunately, it is still much more common that *too little attention* is given to the dying person, rather than too much, and it is here that we should focus our energies. We need to know more than we do about the care of the dying, with emphasis on the patient as a sensitive and sensible human being, and more about how best to help the anxious, strained, and suffering family and friends, during and after the event of dying. Ultimately, good care of the dying will be a test of the teamwork of all involved—family, pastor, medical personnel, et al., so that *persons* can live their last days with self-possession and self-respect whenever humanly possible. This is good stewardship of life.

Clearly the statement does not confront the issue of euthanasia, but perhaps it provides a groundwork for future discussions in harmony with the basic principles in the Statement.

The Moravian Church

The Moravian Church adopted a statement concerning euthanasia at the 1974 Synod, Northern Province. The report, presented by the Committee on Church and Society, supported the use of the Living Will, the refusal by terminally ill patients to the use of heroic treatment, but rejected active euthanasia, which they labelled "mercy killing." The statement read as follows:

WHEREAS: God has conquered death through Christ, and

WHEREAS: this belief is a central affirmation to the faith of a Christian, and is declared through our worship as the Church, the living body of Christ, and

WHEREAS: the resulting resurrection faith of the Christian ought to exemplify a lack of fear in the face of death, therefore be it

RESOLVED: (1) that members of the Moravian Church reaffirm God's message to man about death as spoken by Christ: "I am the resurrection and the life, he who believes in me, though he die, yet shall he live, and whosoever lives and believes in me shall never die." (John 11:25–26) and be it further

RESOLVED: (2) that in handling the subject of the right to die with dignity without heroic life-prolonging measures, faith in Christ's victory shall be the setting in which one speaks of death, and through which we find its ultimate meaning; not as creators of life, but as creatures who believe in the eternal love of our creator.

WHEREAS : science is developing ever-increasing means to prolong life, and

WHEREAS: neither science nor religion have fully understood the mystery of when the physical life of an individual ends, and

WHEREAS: individuals should have the right to predetermine what will happen to them when their death becomes imminent, therefore be it

RESOLVED: (3) that this Synod approve of the practice of allowing an individual to die with dignity.

WHEREAS: it would be helpful to family and attending physician(s) to know the wishes of individuals facing death, therefore be it

RESOLVED: (4) that member of Moravian congregations be encouraged to study documents such as a "Living Will" regarding care when their own death will become imminent and prepare in written form their wishes; and be it further

RESOLVED: (5) that since there are certain diseases which are either deteriorating and/or cause intractable pain, and which will undoubtedly have no known cure at any given period in scientific discoveries, members of the Moravian Church do not condemn those who choose the right to die with dignity without heroic life-prolonging measures or those who are supportive of their decision; and be it further

RESOLVED: (6) that since the physically, mentally, and/or emotionally handicapped persons do receive definite satisfactions from life, this Synod disapproves of "mercy killing" as an appropriate means for dealing with any problems that may surround handicapped persons, and be it further

RESOLVED: (7) that the Board of Christian Education and Evangelism be responsible for the scheduling, planning, and programming of seminars on death and dying, including euthanasia, during the next intersynodal period and provide adequate and appropriate materials and resources for use at the local congregational level.

The Plymouth Brethren

The Plymouth Brethren "have no central organization nor denominational structure," according to James A. Stahr, Executive Director of Letters of Interest Association, publishers of *Interest* magazine. Thus they have "no mechanism by which official positions can be taken on any subject. Each local church is essentially autonomous." However, Mr. Stahr comments:

> After many years of ministry and travel among Plymouth Brethren churches, I think I can safely say that the general consensus would be strongly in favor of the sanctity of life, with resultant opposition to both abortion and euthanasia. However, I know of no discussions that have taken place between local churches on these subjects.
>
> Our churches share a common belief in the soul, the bodily resurrection, and the afterlife in either heaven or hell. Ritual and sanctified burial grounds are not characteristic of our churches. Therefore, funeral services would be unaffected by euthanasia.

The United Church of Christ

On June 25, 1973, the Synod of the United Church of Christ adopted "A Statement of Christian concern addressed to the Churches from the Ninth General Synod." It read, in part:

> Nothing in Jewish or Christian traditions or in medical ethics presumes that a physician has a mandate to impose his or her wishes and skills upon patients for the sake of prolonging the length of their dying where those patients are diagnosed as terminally ill and do not wish the interventions of the physician. People who are dying have as much freedom as other living persons to accept or to refuse medical treatment where that treatment provides no cure for their ailment. Thus the freedom of the patient to choose his/her own style for the remainder of his/her life and the method and time for dying is enhanced. Here the illness, or, depending on one's theology, God, has already made death imminent.

The Statement endorsed the Living Will and recognized that, "It is ethically and theologically proper for a person to wish to avoid artificial and/or painful prolongation of terminal illness and for him or her to execute a living will or similar document of instructions." The Statement went on to note:

> In another situation the patient may be in an irreversible terminal illness, perhaps with substantial pain or physical distress, but in no condition to give instructions and without a previously made living will

99

or document of instructions. Again, life or death itself is no longer a question. The only question is "when." These are patients who would die reasonably soon if given only painkilling treatment but whose body could be kept alive, or at least with functioning organs (heart, lungs) by artificial means. The question is whether extraordinary measures should be used or whether the patient should be allowed to complete his or her natural death.

Every day in hospitals across the land, these decisions are made clinically. Too often they are made covertly. Too many hospitals, doctors and relatives feel vulnerable when facing the issue and so refuse to have the decision-making process open. Some are torn over their own motivation. Some fear they may be violating the will of God. Some fear malpractice suits by a money-seeking heir or ambitious prosecuting attorney.

We believe there comes a time in the course of an irreversible terminal illness when, in the interest of love, mercy and compassion, those who are caring for the patient should say: "Enough." We do not believe simply the continuance of mere physical existence is either morally defensible or social desirable or is God's will.

Concerning suffering and miraculous cures, the Statement read: "While we may learn from suffering, we do not believe it to be the intentional will of God that persons must be so tested," and, "Christians can and do affirm the miraculous acts of God; hope and pray for such acts and yet also know that God's will does not involve suffering beyond the limits of human endurance. God's miracles are beyond human power to control."

On June 27, 1979, the Twelfth General Synod reaffirmed the 1973 Statement and gave public support to and endorsement of the importance and legitimacy of Living Wills.

It is clear that the United Church of Christ supports passive euthanasia; the attitude toward active euthanasia is not stipulated. However, in the query about a terminal patient unable to sign a Living Will the question is left open as to "whether the patient should be allowed to complete his or her natural death." Because the Synod did not specifically outline the implications in this notation, the subject of active euthanasia must be considered *sub judice*, so far as the United Church of Christ is concerned.

Evangelicals

In 1972, The National Association of Evangelicals passed a resolution concerning "Responsibility to the Aging." The third goal in the resolution was: "That each person receive adequate medical attention as needed. In this connection the NAE affirms the right of persons to die with dignity without the use of extraordinary means to prolong biological life. In no case is euthanasia justified."

In 1981, the issue of euthanasia was addressed in a resolution dealing with "A Response to Secular Humanism," which included numerous ethical issues that the NAE believed stemmed from "secular humanism." The statement reads:

The National Association of Evangelicals alerts its constituency to the fact that—secular humanism has infiltrated the life of our nation, the structure of our families, the classrooms of our educational institutions, the ethical practices of our society, and it is often sapping the vital life of our religious faith. The proponents of secular humanism have set for themselves the monumental task of dissuading people from a belief in God, in His Word and in His moral commandments. Such humanists claim that belief in God and His moral law is the highest form of self-deception; hence the world would be better off without God. As a result, men and women stand above God in the universe and develop nonbiblical views about abortion, sexual permissiveness, easy divorce, genetic engineering and euthanasia, which views contradict the claims of secular humanists that they are committed to "the shared joys of family life, love, work, and career . . . to compassionate concern for the entire community of humankind."

The statement continued with a contrast between the positions of the Humanists—as analyzed by the NAE—and the NAE affirmation of faith. The penultimate paragraph returned to the issue of euthanasia:

Thus, as evangelical Christians, we declare that biblical sexual morality is binding and not relative to human desires as in the new morality; that the life-long bond of marriage is the will of God and that divorce is not for the Christian family ; and that the rights of the unborn child are sacred and not to be determined by personal desires of the parents; that human life is a gift of God and no one has the right to tamper with it in *euthanasia* or genetic engineering.

Swedenborgianism

The Church of the New Jerusalem (Swedenborgian) stands somewhat outside of traditional Western religions in that it recognizes a new "Divine revelation of truth given by the Lord Jesus Christ through His servant Emanuel Swedenborg" (*The General Church of the New Jerusalem: A Handbook of General Information*, 1952, p. 3). Swedenborg is recognized by the Church as an 18th century (1688–1722) "human instrument" of revelation.

The questionnaire was answered by the Rev. Michael D. Gladish, pastor of the Gabriel Church of the New Jerusalem in La Crescenta, California. Pastor Gladish wrote in response to the questions:

1

OUR CHURCH'S STAND ON
"PASSIVE" EUTHANASIA:

From our doctrine we understand that all life is of and from God, and flows into the human "vessel" according to the organic, physiological and spiritual conditions that apply. Thus life flows into and is received by minerals, vegetables and animals each in a different way. The purpose of human life or consciousness is that God's love and wisdom be received AS IF THEY WERE our own, so that not only do we

103

have consciousness but *self*-consciousness in the exercise of free will and rationality.

The faculties of will and understanding are opened and developed as a result of the interaction between sense experience and spiritual influx. Everything in the organic body corresponds to one or the other of these faculties, and the principal organs are the heart—which corresponds to the will—and the lungs—which corresponds to the understanding. When the heart and the lungs can no longer function as of themselves and the brain no longer registers any responsiveness to either internal or external stimulation we take these as indications that the uniquely human quality of life has been withdrawn by God from that form; in other words, the spirit has departed and whatever life remains is not human life but life on a lower plane —with which we are relatively free to do as we like.

As a church organization we do not "sanction" much of anything on an external level, but try to represent the teachings about spiritual life as well as we can so that individuals in their best judgments can decide about issues of application. Thus an individual member of our organization might choose to sustain life in a human body by various "heroic" measures for various personal reasons (and I know of one such case), but on the other hand I do not know any ministers in our organization who would condemn the act of "passive euthanasia" as you have described it.

2

OUR CHURCH'S STAND ON
"ACTIVE" EUTHANASIA:

I do not know of any ministers in our organization who would sanction any form of suicide or other "active euthanasia" such as you have described.

Human life does not consist of what happens to us but is rather a conscious response through the will and the understanding TO whatever happens to us. The experience of Norman Cousins (made famous in the book, *Anatomy of an Illness*) is a classic modern example of how the mind or spirit can overcome the adversities of the flesh. Jesus also taught that the spirit gives life, the flesh profits nothing (John 6:63) and that in the world we would have tribulation but through Him we might still have peace and be of good cheer (John 16:33). As tragic as human circumstances may be—and I am well aware that they may be terribly tragic—I believe an individual must persevere.

Now if the flesh "profits nothing" you may wonder why we won't condone a deliberate rejection of it—for the enhanced spiritual life this might facilitate. In response, I enclose a sheet concerning the duration of life on earth. . . . We are given the natural circumstances of our lives within which to grow spiritually, and we cannot become truly spiritual except through the effort—however feeble and restricted it may be—to exercise our faculties of choice in favor of whatever God-given virtue might be possible: I think of courage, for example, and honesty and optimism, not to mention faith, conscience, innocence and obedience of the 10 commandments, which includes the law against murder.

Of course, we would not object to the use of medicines to ease pain or in other ways make hard circumstances easier to bear, but on the other hand I don't know of anyone in the church who would condone the use of drugs permanently to obstruct the exercise of the mental faculties. That would be much the same as taking the human life, since it would take the humanity out of that life.

Incidentally, one of the great difficulties in the decision about active euthanasia in any particular case is the very question of mental competence. I believe, and in my conscience I would have to advocate, that if we err we must err on the positive side, assuming there is truly human value not only to the suffering person but also through him to others in the continuation of his life. After all, human value is not determined by appearance.

And finally, once active euthanasia is condoned by law or conscience there is an awesome burden of responsibility to define justifiable circumstances. I don't think we can do this fairly *ever* and so must rest with the Word and Providence of God. Too much is at stake: too much that we in our limited perspective can't see.

By the way, in condemning the ACT of "active" euthanasia we do not condemn an individual who commits it. Though we believe the reasoning of someone who does this is impaired, false or misguided, we do not believe anyone but God can see the heart of another human being and we leave that judgment to Him. Spiritually speaking, the heart or motive of an act always qualifies it for the doer.

3

BELIEF IN A SOUL OR AFTERLIFE:

YES, with judgment according to the interior quality of the life, not by edict (Divine or otherwise) but according to the law of consequences: and spiritual association. An evil man, for instance, is already in hell, being influenced and surrounded by the evils he enjoys *and* the evil spirits who are like-minded. A good man is already in heaven, being in a heavenly state, and the transition from this world to the next is simply a matter of awakening consciousness on a new plane or level. We are not rewarded or punished for *things* we have done on earth, but the interior state of our life is simply continued, evil if evil, including the torments of frustration, the fires of anger and passion, jealousy, etc., and wonderful if good, including the sense of peace that can be cultivated even in spite of pain, through faith and humility.

With my conscience if I participated in euthanasia I would expect to bear the consequences in the form of spiritual torment; however, everything depends upon the interior quality of the motive, thus also the degree in which I have been able to exercise a truly free choice. If I have felt compelled by the pressure of outside circumstances so that I did not see even my own principles clearly any more, then I have hope that God's mercy will restore better judgment later and that being for-given I may come to forgive myself and live in spiritual peace.

4

FUNERAL CUSTOMS FOR THE
VICTIMS OF MERCY KILLING:

No differences from others. In the case of suicide we try to give the benefit of the doubt as to mental competence, not holding the individual responsible for a free and rational choice to commit murder. But in the last analysis who can place blame spiritually but God? As to our services we usually go to the site of burial (or cremation) first, and commit the body, then we proceed to the church for a "memorial" or "resurrection" service in which we focus on our teachings concerning the afterlife and on the positive qualities of the deceased person's life, eulogizing but not glorifying the individual and leaving judgment to God.

5

COUNSELING FOR
SOMEONE
CONTEMPLATING
EUTHANASIA/SUICIDE?

Focus first on acknowledgment and acceptance of the feelings expressed so that the person gains a sense of worth through acceptance and real communication. Gradually and very gently try to instill some concepts of use, especially spiritual use, and a perspective of human values beyond (yet within the context of) the physical limitations that apply. Listening, active listening, would be the primary skill to exercise, for this more than anything highlights the value of continued life, which consists of nothing so much as communication. The essence of human life is love and if love cannot share it cannot go on.

6

SCRIPTURAL OR DOCTRINAL
REFERENCES?

I'm sorry but I do not have time for the extensive research that this would entail right now. However, our doctrinal point of view is taken specifically from the theological, exegetical and eschatological writings of Emanuel Swedenborg (1688–1772), some 30 volumes which may be found in many libraries. See especially the work on *Divine Providence* and the one on *Heaven and Hell* by Swedenborg. His work on *The New Jerusalem and Its Heavenly Doctrine* also provides insights into our understanding of the human spirit in relation to the body, as does the small treatment, *Divine Love and Divine Wisdom* found at the end of the 6th volume of *Apocalypse Explained*.

The Seventh Day Adventists

According to Dr. Mervyn G. Hardinge, Director of the Health and Temperance Department of the General Conference of Seventh Day Adventists, the denomination has undertaken no research to date on the subject of euthanasia. Indeed, Dr. Jim Walters, Assistant Professor of Christian Ethics at Loma Linda University, California, commented that "one would think that a denomination as heavily involved in health care as ours is" would have engaged in such a study. However, "an informal consensus appears to exist among S.D.A. clinicians and theologians in favor of passive euthanasia in at least some cases" according to Dr. David Larson of Loma Linda University. "The religious rationale is that it is both pointless and cruel to prolong the process of dying for no justifiable reasons."

Dr. Gerald R. Winslow, Professor of Religion at Walla Walla College in College Place, Washington, has been specializing in biomedical ethics "for the past nine or ten years." In response to the first question in the questionnaire, he wrote:

I know of no moral or theological positions espoused by Adventists that would prevent this patient's physician from ordering the termination of artificial life-support. I believe that most Adventist physicians would be willing to so act if they were reasonably certain that continuing artificial life-support would be futile. Personally, I would hope that the family could be involved in the decision to terminate what appear from

108

this brief description to be unreasonable measures to sustain life. But assuming that this patient's brain is "gone" meaning a persistent vegetative state is an accurate description of the facts, then there is no moral or theological obligation known to Adventists that would require further life-supporting effort.

Dr. Jack Provensha, who is both a medical doctor and an ethicist at the Loma Linda University Center for Christian Bioethics, responding to the first question in the questionnaire, believes that the Seventh Day Adventists would sanction the removal of life-support systems for someone whose brain "was gone" and who would die without the system:

The person is defined functionally by SDA's. The above individual had suffered "personal death," even if he has not yet technically suffered brain death. The "meaning" of "active" and "passive" euthanasia differs for those who administer it. The difference being one of "causal" participation in the event. Letting nature take its course is not the same as giving nature a boost. We are concerned about protecting the sensitivities for life in the care provided but not meaninglessly. Heroics in the above case would be meaningless.

Concerning the case of M in question #2, Professor Winslow wrote:

Again, Adventists have not taken an official position. But my educated hunch is that Adventists do not differ from the mainstream of Christian thought on this subject. Most denominations, and Adventists are no exception, are against suicide. Suicide is viewed by Adventists as a breaking of one of God's commandments. But this still leaves open the question whether or not every case of "active euthanasia" carried out with the patient's consent or carried out by the patient him/herself counts as wrongful suicide. My own position is that health care providers should not conduct active euthanasia, and I am quite sure that nearly all, if not all, Adventist practitioners would concur. No state in the union allows for active euthanasia, the AMA does not permit it, and there are good reasons beyond the conventions of laws or professional ethics to establish a strong moral presumption against active euthanasia being conducted by the medical profession. I believe that active euthanasia if practiced by physicians and nurses would seriously alter for the worse the ethos of medicine. I notice that those like Dame Saunders and Dr. Kübler-Ross who have probably gained the most experience in helping the dying are generally opposed to active euthanasia. But what about the patient in your case who may take an overdose? Personally, I do not think that we should do all in our power to prevent such an occurrence. Nor should there be criminal penalties for attempting suicide in such cases.

Dr. Provensha believes also that his denomination would not favor M taking her own life:

Recognizing that pain can be depersonalizing as can drugs, the SDA physician would try to balance the drugs against the pain in such a way as to maximize insofar as possible what personhood remains. The patient may still pull it off but the physician should be guided by his person-protective ideals in the care he prescribes. It is personal life that has value and as long as it persists it should be protected. The issue is the quality of life, not mere biological life. The health care provider who values personal existence will do what he can to preserve it. The alternative is open to all kinds of abuse.

Nor would Seventh Day Adventists approve of assisted suicide for the terminally ill. Dr. Larson comments, "There is a strong, though informal presumption against deliberately destroying human life." Dr. Provensha expanded the idea. "Personal life is precious as a gift of God and must not be rejected casually. The patient has the right to do what we may think is wrong but not the right to have others violate their moral standards in assisting her." He continued: "Self destruction is wrong whether assisted or not and whether compassionate or not. Compassion should be directed toward supportive care and pain control."

Dr. Winslow also believes that the SDA church would not approve of assisted suicide or "compassionate murder." Concerning the latter, he wrote:

I believe that my church would oppose such action as wrongful on the grounds that human beings should not arrogate to themselves the power to end life which belongs only to God. (Adventists, it should be noted, tend to be pacifists for much the same reasons.) But I should hasten to add that physicians should be free to provide sufficient dosages of pain relievers so that the patients can be kept as free of pain as possible even if this results in the unintended shortening of life in some cases.

Adventists believe in an afterlife and in judgment. "SDA's do not believe in the Platonic immortal soul," wrote Dr. Provensha, "but do believe in a resurrection at the end of the world. They also believe in divine judgment based not on single acts such as compulsive suicide, however, but in the general relationship with God. A rational, calculated, self-destructive act would be considered to reflect an unfortunate and broken relationship with the life-giver." Professor Walters noted that "If active euthanasia were deemed as murder (of the self) then this 'Sin' would obviously count against one in the judgment." Professor Winslow wrote: "Adventists do not believe in the immortality of the soul. The Adventist view is that human beings are souls in their wholeness. At death the person 'sleeps'—to use the biblical metaphor. So far as I know there is no Adventist position on what effect participation in euthanasia would have on eternal destiny. But it should be noted that Adventists believe in salvation by grace alone and not by works."

So far as euthanasia affecting the burial rituals, Professor Walters states, "Adventists are not heavily liturgical; and what liturgy pertains to a funeral service applies to saint and sinner alike. The difference would appear in what is said (or not said!) in the funeral sermon." Dr. Provensha suggests that, "It might condition the attitudes of mourners who might feel more sorrowful about the death. But no difference would be made in the rituals, etc."

Concerning counseling, Dr. Winston wrote, "I hope and I believe that Adventists would seek to help those who, for example, want to sign a Living Will. My own counsel would be that we should never seek to end by direct action the life of any human being, but we should be willing to stop medical treatment that seems futile." Professor Walters thinks, "It would depend upon the local pastor. Possibly pastoral counseling—or psychological, and the direction it would take (pro or con euthanasia) would be decided by the pastor involved."

Dr. Larson suggests that four aspects of counseling would be important: to "listen," to "sort out as many options as possible," to "encourage deliberateness, not speed," and to "invite people to make up their own minds responsibly." Dr. Provensha thinks that the counseling "would be in the direction of helping the persons counseled to accept the true status of the one dying. This would apply to 'K.' For one still personally alive it would have to do with providing information requisite for deciding to reject treatment alternatives. Also some attempt to instil in such a person a sense of value for what life remained. It would allow the person to make his or her final judgment, however." With regard to counseling and "active euthanasia," Dr. Provensha believes it would counsel against it as an immoral act of self destruction—and would try to instil a sense of respect for life—even if limited. The only biblical passage quoted by Dr. Provensha was "Thou shalt not kill."

The Mormons

Mr. Glenn N. Rowe, Manager of Public Services of the Historical Department of the Church of Jesus Christ of Latter-Day Saints (Mormon), was unable to provide answers to the specific questions in the survey. He did share a statement from "the Church's current *General Handbook of Instructions,* published in 1983, and intended as a book of guidelines for local Church leadership," and another brief comment on euthanasia, by Dr. James O. Mason, former Commissioner of Health Services for the Church. The statement from the Handbook is as follows:

> Because of its belief in the dignity of life, the Church opposes euthanasia. In addition to faith in the Lord, members should call upon recognized and licensed medical practitioners to assist in reversing conditions that threaten life. When dying becomes inevitable, it should be considered a blessing and a purposeful part of mortality.

Dr. Mason's statement is in a list of items under the title "Attitudes of The Church of Jesus Christ of Latter-Day Saints Toward Certain Medical Problems." The section titled "Prolongation of Life and Right to Die" reads:

> The Church does not look with favor upon any form of mercy killing. It believes in the dignity of life; faith in the Lord and medical science should be appropriately called upon and applied to reverse conditions that are a threat to life. There comes a time when dying becomes inevitable, when it should be looked upon as a blessing, and as a purposeful part of mortality.

113

Christian Science

Mr. Al M. Carnesciali responded to our request for information on behalf of the Christian Science Committee on Publication for Southern California. He wrote:

As Christian Scientists, we recognize that prolonged illness, issues of aging, and euthanasia are widespread problems in today's society.

As a rule, our Church does not establish official denominational positions on the broad range of social and personal issues. *The Christian Science Monitor,* which is published by The Christian Science Publishing Society, however, deals with vital social questions on a continuing basis; but it does not represent Church policy or official denominational stands. Church members are free to determine their own positions on such questions according to individual conscience, prayerful striving, and moral judgment.

Rather than our returning a completed questionnaire, I believe it would be most helpful to give some insight on how a Christian Scientist would view this subject. Euthanasia in particular is one subject that can be discussed only within the context of medical practice, since it involves acceptance of the incurability of particular diseases and the assumption that an individual is doomed in certain instances. On the other hand, Christian Scientists view the question of living and dying from a religious standpoint and rely on spiritual means for healing. They accept the fact that Jesus cured many diseases that were considered incurable and expected his followers to do the same.

114

A Christian Scientist does not consider any disease beyond the power of God to heal. For this reason, he would not be an advocate of euthanasia. Christian Scientists realize the complexity of this issue within the context of ordinary medical practice, however. Also, while Christian Scientists strive to follow Jesus' commands and to fulfill his promise of abundant life, they recognize, like all Christians, how far they still have to go in this regard. And they feel only the deepest compassion for those faced with the dilemma they may feel when struggling with pain and disease, either Christian Scientists or others.

Jehovah's Witnesses

In response to our questionnaire, the Watchtower Bible and Tract Society of New York, Inc. (Jehovah's Witnesses) shared copies of two articles on euthanasia that appeared in their magazine *Awake!*. The first, entitled "What About 'Mercy Killing'?", was published May 8, 1974, and the second, "Mercy Killing," on March 8, 1978. Both articles reflect an awareness of the inherent difficulties in cases where an individual is dying from a painful, incurable illness.

Active euthanasia is forbidden on three grounds. First, it violates the commandment "You must not murder" (Exodus 20:13). Second, it violates "the Bible's command that Christians 'hold a good conscience'" (1 Pet. 3:16). In discussing this point, the article refers to comments by Robert S. Morison in *Scientific American*, 1973, where he states that "an overwhelming majority of physicians, and certainly a substantial majority of laymen, instinctively recoil from such active measures as prescribing a known poison or injecting a large bubble into a vein." Third, Christians are required to "be in subjection to superior authorities" (Romans 13:1), and obey the laws of the land. And, in Jehovah's Witness thinking, active euthanasia is murder. Because they respect God's view of the sanctity of life, out of regard for their own consciences and in obedience to governmental laws, those desiring to conform their lives to Bible principles would never resort to positive euthanasia (*Awake!*, May 8, 1978, p. 28).

116

The Jehovah's Witnesses do not oppose passive euthanasia. "However, where there is clear evidence that death is imminent and unavoidable, the Scriptures do not require that extraordinary (and perhaps costly) means be employed to stretch out the dying process. In such a case, allowing death to take its course uninhibited would not violate any law of God. However, there is need for caution before people decide that a patient is beyond all hope of recovery" (*Awake!*, March 8, 1978, p. 7).

It should be noted that Jehovah's Witnesses believe they "are now living in the 'conclusion' or 'the last days' of the present system of things (Matt. 24:3–34; 2 Tim. 3:1–5). This means that God's new order will become a reality within this generation." This "new order" means that "not only will people no longer become sick, but those who are now afflicted with infirmities will be permanently healed" (Isa. 33:24; 35:5–7) (*Awake!*, May 8, 1974, p. 28).

Although Jehovah's Witnesses do not shun medical assistance in time of illness, they do refuse blood transfusions outside of auto transfusions—which refers to blood donated by the person him/herself and frozen for possible use by the donor at a later date. The refusal to accept blood donated by others rests in the interpretation of biblical passages commanding that animal flesh with its blood not be eaten (Gen. 9:3–6; Leviticus 17:11–14; and the prohibition in Acts 15:28–29). For the Witnesses, intravenous injection is a form of feeding on blood. Witnesses do not interpret the refusal to accept transfusions as acts of martyrdom or, should the patient die, as suicide. According to William L. Barry, a Jehovah's Witness official: "They consider their integrity and witness to God's law more important. They have confidence in the resurrection and God's reward for them" (reported by Russell Chandler, "Rather Die Than Take Blood—Witnesses," *The Los Angeles Times*, August 20, 1977).

Unitarians

The Unitarian Universalist Association is composed of "independent member churches and fellowships, each of which establishes its own statement of purposes," according to Donald W. Male, secretary. Mary O. Rosa, Associate Director of the Section on Social Responsibility, shared a copy of the resolution on "The Legality of Living Wills," which was passed by the 1978 General Assembly. She also responded to the questionnaire.

The resolution affirmed the right of individuals "to decide the nature of their care during terminal illness," affirmed and defended the "right of each person to sign a legally binding Living Will," and called upon members to support legislation affirming the legality of such documents.

Mary Rosa wrote that:

> No position has yet been taken by the General Assembly on active euthanasia. However, the Social Responsibility Section at UUA Headquarters, working with the Committee of Aging of the UUA Board of Trustees, maintains contact with such organizations as Concern for Dying and the Hemlock Society and makes their materials available to interested UU societies and individuals.

The Association would take no stand on assisted suicide. Because there is no expressed belief in afterlife, the answer to question #3 of my survey would be "a matter of individual belief." She adds:

"A belief common among UUs, however, is that this mortal existence is what we have and that it is our right and responsibility to
develop its fullest potential for ourselves and for all of humanity."

Rituals associated with death would not be affected if death came
through euthanasia, and would not "diminish our celebration of
the life that has ended or our caring support of the deceased person's
family and friends." The counseling provided would be determined
by the individual clergy working with the person involved.

Baptist Churches

Baptist Churches are independent units. It is not surprising that neither the Baptist World Alliance, a voluntary fellowship of 127 conventions/unions worldwide, nor the North American Baptist Fellowship have taken stands on euthanasia. Nor, according to Robert D. Hughes, Executive Director, has the Southern Baptist Convention. No discussions have taken place in the meetings of the Evangelical Baptist Church, Inc., according to Miss Clyde M. Dawson, Administrative Secretary. Philip R. Bryan reports that the Baptist Missionary Association of America has not taken an official stand on any of the issues in the questionnaire.

Glen O. Spence, Executive Secretary of the General Association of General Baptists, provided the following statement from the denomination's *Social Principles Booklet,* which is the generally accepted position on euthanasia:

> Termination of Life: We believe life and death belong in the hands of God. Regardless of circumstances that befall man, he must know that God gave him existence and He holds him responsible for his stewardship of life. We are thankful to medical science for efforts and accomplishments made in preventing disease and illness and for the great advances in treatment which extend the life and usefulness of those afflicted. It is of deep Christian concern, however, when people suffer from incurable diseases to the point where the wisdom of God is questioned in continuing life. Questions arise as to whether a person has the right to die if it means release from suffering. The deliberate

120

termination of life is a serious concern, whether it be done by the person himself, a friend, or the physician. We oppose euthanasia, sometimes referred to as mercy killing. We feel the answer is to be found in faith, endurance and communication with God. We endorse the removal of pain by the use of drugs, even though consciousness may be lost because of it. We affirm the right of every person to die with dignity. We reject efforts made to prolong terminal illnesses merely because the technology is available to do so. At the same time we endorse the work and discoveries made by medical science through scientific experimentation based upon accepted procedures. However, the physician has the responsibility to insure that every precaution is taken so the patient is in no way victimized by such experimentation or its products.

The Rev. Leon M. Maltby, Chairman of the Christian Social Action Committee of the Seventh Day Baptist General Convention, wrote: "To the best of my knowledge euthanasia has not come up for serious study by our committee nor have there been conference pronouncements on the subject." He suggests that the reason the subject has not been discussed is that "practically none of our people favor it. It is too 'far out' to be seriously considered by Christians of the Seventh Day Baptist variety. We believe, I think, that only non-Christians favor it. If there is a real danger that the idea is gaining momentum and is likely to become prevalent, then we, as SDB's, should join with others in opposing it."

Mr. Maltby indicated that it would be difficult to respond on behalf of his denomination to the questionnaire: "Ours is a democratic (congregational) denomination. It is hard to get consensus on hard questions in one church, much less in all."

Paul D. Simmons of the Southern Baptist Seminary, in the Summer 1977 issue of *Perspectives in Religious Studies,* which is published by the Association of Baptist Professors of Religion, contributed an article titled "Death with Dignity: Christians Confront Euthanasia" (pp. 112–159). The article raises issues discussed earlier in our study and concludes:

> One can expect that any conclusion reached on the subject of the Christian's confronting euthanasia will also entail a degree of ambiguity. While this may seem indecisive to some, it will have the salutory effect

of not simplistically resolving a complicated matter. Several things can be said by way of conclusion. First, the right to die with dignity can be supported with equal vigor as the responsibility for the medical care of the ill. The wishes of those who desire not to be sustained beyond responsive personhood are to be respected as firmly as the wishes of those who wish to be sustained as long as medically possible.

Second, those who elect death by "direct and voluntary" means may be seen as acting in the context of the Christian freedom to choose the terms under which they are to die. Suicide of this type is hardly to be regarded as a sin for which there is no forgiveness. On the contrary, such a decision may be based upon a commitment to the truth that "whether we live or whether we die, we are the Lord's" (Rom. 14:8).

Third, Christians may well work to mollify the legal penalties that may be imposed upon those who act decisively to relieve loved ones of unbearable suffering. At the same time, they will work diligently to assure that such decisions must not be borne by one isolated from the physical-family health care team. No one person should have to bear the mental and spiritual burden of deciding when a patient should be enabled to die.

Finally, Christians should be actively engaged in the discussions of the issues involved in euthanasia. The debate between a "sanctity of life ethic" and a "quality of life ethic" raises substantive questions for Christian theology. The biblical witness sustains a great hope in life that cannot be simply identified with biological functions. It is in the context of that hope that all discussions of death must be placed. For, as the Apostle reminded his readers, "If for this life only we have hoped in Christ, we are of all men most to be pitied" (I Cor. 15:19).

The Theosophical Society

The teachings of the Theosophical Society rest primarily upon the works of Madame Helen P. Blavatsky who founded the organization in New York City in 1875. The organization did not respond directly to the questionnaire but sent a copy of *Report of the European Tour, May 20–July 15, 1980* (Theosophical University Press, 1980). This volume provides edited lectures and conversations of Grace F. Knoche, Leader of the Society, taped during a tour of Europe and Great Britain. Miss Knoche responds to questions concerning euthanasia and beliefs in the afterlife (among other things) which touch upon the questions in the questionnaire.

In her opening remarks in Munich, Miss Knoche delineated the Society's beliefs concerning the importance of Madame Blavatsky's teachings (p. 6). She stated that, not only had the founder presented "ancient truths that had been given to mankind long ages ago . . . but she did so with the chief aim of restoring dignity to the human race." Miss Knoche continued:

> We had forgotten who we were; we had overlooked the fact that we are *gods in essence*. We had buried our heritage under creeds, and she restored to us the knowledge that we are transcendent beings, cosmic in power, using human vehicles for experience. When we realize what that means in our daily lives we see that there isn't a single avenue of experience or duty that cannot be viewed from the eyes of our cosmic

self. This is extraordinarily important, because we recognize then that
we are gods, first and foremost, divinities temporarily *using* human
bodies. In other words, we are literally exiles from our real selves, and
that puts quite a new perspective on our experience here on earth. We
know that, whatever our karma, we need never be overwhelmed, because the *long* perspective, the long avenue of experience, gives us a
sense of unlimited resources on which we can draw.

When she was asked a question about the destiny of the individual "divine being" after death, she replied:

Briefly put, when we die, the body is cast off and, the highest having
gone to its own parent star, we are left with the spiritual essence of
ourselves and our human attributes, both higher and lower, in an en-
velope, as it were. After a brief period of unconsciousness, we enter a
purgation state, a cleansing process in which all that is heavy and material and low drops off, while the aroma or essence of all that was fine
and noble in the life is drawn up into the spiritual self of us and enters
a type of heaven-world—we call it devachan, which simply means "god-
place"—there to enter the Elysian Fields, as the Greeks would say, in
order to experience the fulfillment of its aspirations. This is a beautiful
period in which all that has happened in the life, spiritually, has an
opportunity to impress itself on the soul, while the spiritual monad in
which the human entity is sleeping enters the planetary spheres for its
own higher adventures. The old Latins made effective use of the epitaph:
Dormit in astris, "he sleeps among the stars" and also: *Gaudeat in
astris,* "he rejoices among the stars." In those two simple statements is
an epitome of the theosophic teaching: a part of us *is* sleeping among
the stars, and yet, during our dream-sleep, a still higher part of us is
rejoicing in the freedom of sending forth its consciousness among the
planetary and solar realms.

To return to your question: Where does our god-spark, or inner god,
go when we die? It is a paradox: our god essence never leaves its own
sphere and yet, because it is our essential self, it protects us from its
own lofty sphere. *We* have to grow up as human beings into our godlike
qualities; it is *we* who must approach their realm. But there is no
separation unless we, through lives of direct deliberate evildoing, break
the link.

In Manchester, England, she commented on "the right to die with dignity" (p. 146):

> There is a movement abroad, among doctors and the general public, to allow people the "right to die in dignity," and the right to die when the soul is ready, and not keep the body going by artificial means. There is a moment when the soul knows that it is time to quit the body. We may not know the moment, it may be weeks in coming, but there should be an atmosphere of welcoming the change called death, recognizing that it is a beneficent process, that it is part of the pattern of the total life-experience that continues far longer than this immediate lifetime.

In response to a question concerning the use of the phrase "the right to die" by groups in Britain "who are claiming the right for euthanasia" she responded:

> I am not referring to euthanasia. What I am speaking of is this: I believe that we should allow the *soul* to decide—by which I mean the higher soul, and not our brain-mind—because I believe it is wrong to take life. If we understood more we would know when to let go of our bodies, but we have lost that innate knowledge. There is a time to let the body go, and even in our Western culture there are many who do know this intuitively.
>
> Some of the traditional peoples have retained this knowledge. In Nigeria they speak of death as "losing one's hold on mortality." I heard this story directly from the son of a chief who was over 100. The chief called together his large family or clan, and told them he would soon be leaving them. He gave them a long and beautiful talk about the spiritual principles that guided his life and the sacred tradition of his people. Then he entered the dying process: his consciousness went up and came down again, and he spoke to them. Three times this happened. Then he gave a final blessing and was gone. There is great beauty in this. He knew the time had come to "lose his hold on mortality."
>
> Such intuitive knowledge hopefully will come back to us when we regain the "child state" that we have lost in our sophistication and in our hunger to live, to grasp, to gain. But this is *not* euthanasia. We should *not* take life. As Cicero and other Greek and Latin poets and philosophers always said, the soul is "the possession of the gods"—the

divine within—and therefore is on a tour of duty; we have no right to dispose of our lives before the direction comes from above-within. This is the message that has been given by the wise of all ages.

At a Members Meeting in London, Miss Knoche talked about the Society's belief in Karma and reincarnation. She was asked a question about the benefits of "healing circles" in which people " . . . sit and think and pray perhaps for particular people." She replied (p. 179):

I am not so certain that it can do only good. I have experienced the illness and death of many close friends, and often I have thought to myself, "If only I had the power to heal; if only I could bring relief." As I have grown older I have come to realize that that is not the most compassionate way to help another. I have come to understand that the most beautiful and effective way to sustain another is to help him find the courage and the love and the confidence to meet his karma creatively. Of course, we should use all the medical aids that are normally available, but let's allow our friend the honor and the dignity that belong to him, of recognizing that he has the capacity to meet his karma with full knowledge. Maybe his body will die earlier than the norm, but in so meeting the karma that is his, acting with full dignity as a man, he is accepting consciously the privilege of working through a heavy karmic experience for a beneficent purpose. I have seen this work; there is solace and strength in being able to take this attitude.

So, when someone you love dearly is facing death, I myself would not pray to have that one saved at all costs. Rather I would pray—and pray is a good word—for the strength and the love to assist and sustain that friend through his Gethsemane. He (or she) must be allowed to go through that Gethsemane alone, without interference, so that when he has succeeded, he is blessed in having come through in triumph; he has found a new birth of the soul which nothing can take from him henceforth. It is then his victory, not somebody else's.

Ethical Culture
and Humanism

Because of the structure of the organizations, no individual can answer for either the Humanist organizations or the Ethical Culture Societies. Fred Arden, President of the American Ethical Union, notes that individuals "have taken a stand." He wrote that "Jerome Nathanson, then Chairman of the Board of Leaders, New York Society for Ethical Culture, and Algernon D. Black, Fraternity of Leaders, American Ethical Union, were among the signers of 'A Plea for Beneficent Euthanasia' which was published in *The Humanist* magazine (July/August, 1974)." This "Plea" was reprinted in *Beneficent Euthanasia,* edited by Marvin Kohl, (Prometheus Books, 1975). Algernon Black, in an address given to the New York Society for Ethical Culture on March 3, 1963, and subsequently before other Societies, said:

> If we had a more ethical world, we would be able to help one another live, and we would be able to help one another die. We would not be afraid, and we would trust one another because there would be love among us. When there is great love in life and great love at death, we may help one another face death without fear. When human beings have lived to the full, death may be less of a tragedy. And under certain circumstances, death may be a release and a blessing for ourselves or for those we love.

127

The advocates of euthanasia are not callous to the value of human life. They are sensitive and care about safeguarding life. Indeed, because they treasure life, they believe that euthanasia is a problem concerning which human beings must not evade moral responsibility. We dare not be party to the needless and continued suffering of thousands who may wish for and be permitted to have release from suffering. Nor can we ignore the fact that some form of euthanasia is practiced every day by physicians with and without the approval of patients and relatives—where patients are permitted to die—and where the practice is carried on in accord with the physician's conscience and without the benefit of public knowledge or responsible social approval or permission.

We who are associated in the Ethical Movement, and many other people as well, do not look back 3,000 or 2,000 years for final answers on contemporary problems or specific questions of ethics. We know that there is wisdom there, and much of what is valid in our lives, much of our wisdom and sense of values has grown out of the Jewish-Christian tradition. But our whole approach is present-oriented and future-oriented. In addition to past experience, our own experience must help us grow and learn so that we understand better what it means to be human, and what it means to have responsible relations with other human beings and what it means to deal with such questions. This is difficult.

There is in the nature of the universe a being born and dying. It is part of the whole life cycle in this universe. Traditional religions will say God gives and God takes away. We should accept pregnancy and birth, and we should accept death as the will of the power which created and rules the world. Those of us who do not accept this interpretation of man's relation to the processes of existence have to find some way of thinking about this too. True, there may be a time for being born and a time for dying. We know that though man may prolong his life through science, we still have a limited existence and none of us will achieve immortal existence or life eternal, even though we can live longer than men did years ago. But when the time comes when a person is dying, we should not prolong his dying. There is a difference between prolonging life when it still has the qualities of life and prolonging the agony and the processes of death.

The issue is not merely that of the avoidance of pain. It is concerned with the deeper questions of man's attitude toward the responsibility for living and safeguarding life—and the issues involved with what men owe one another. The will to live carries with it the will to bear pain . . . .

Men know that they cannot live without pain any more than they can live without pleasure. . . . One can stand a great deal of pain if there is reason for wanting to live and a basis for hope.

We accept pain as an inevitable part of life. . . . Where there is great love, there can be a will to live that can carry people through great pain.

But there is a point where you and I might want to die, and there might be nothing cowardly or undignified about it because we know that pain from then on is pointless, and there is no hope . . . . We are speaking about freedom here, spiritual freedom . . . the right of an individual to decide how he lives and how he will die. Usually we do not have much control about when and where and how it will happen, but where possible, do we not owe it to one another to try to assure that right?

In a separate, and perhaps more recent statement, Algernon Black wrote:

The will to live is strong in human beings. The capacity to endure suffering is beyond belief. It is part of the human condition that men must endure pain and suffering. To summon strength and courage to endure and overcome such hardships is the test of character. Human dignity requires that men accept the hard realities of life and learn to live with them. Temporary suffering, even though extreme, we must all bear at times. We may hold ourselves to this viewpoint and hope we shall have the strength to withstand suffering.

Since the act of ending a life means the ending of a personality as a conscious, active, unique entity, no effort should be spared to encourage the will of the sufferer to live, to ease his pain by therapy and anesthesia, and to give the quality of nursing care and increased attention and love that will nourish the will to live and the feeling of being loved and wanted. Every possible device should be used to make certain that no one end his existence or be helped to do so because of fear or temporary depression.

Euthanasia originates in man's concern for his fellowman and his compassion for one who is suffering unbearably. For there are times when the margin of pleasure may lessen to the zero point and the margin of pain may increase to the unbearable point. Where the disease has permeated the entire body and the suffering is beyond relief and the agony is such that the individual cannot function, cannot control himself physically or mentally—indeed, where he is reduced to nothingness; where medical science has no remedy and, as far as is known, the illness is terminal and hopeless—in such a case, who has the right to refuse to yield to the request that a person end his misery? As free men, we have a right to live and a right to die.

In many cases the medical profession feels the obligation to keep a human being alive, even when everything indicates the case to be hopeless. Thus life is prolonged when life is no life. Chemicals, food, oxygen, and drugs are pumped into patients, thus prolonging the agony of patients and relatives and adding expense and debts—to little purpose. To continue these efforts is no kindness.

When a relative or friend or professional person is party to an act of euthanasia, every effort should be made to remove this act from the category of criminal action subject to criminal punishment—*provided* the suffering is unbearable and the illness terminal and hopeless, *and* the sufferer has fervently requested such action in the presence of witnesses, *and* written and sworn affidavits are furnished.

Since euthanasia is an act that is irrevocable and irreparable, it must *not* be permitted without the safeguards that protect human beings from personal hostility or prejudices, religious, ethnic, national, and political. It must be protected from purposes of personal gain and fraud, from criminal purposes, and from personal hostility and destructiveness. Since it is born of compassion and love, it must be safeguarded as the deepest possible expression of such compassion—to spare a loved one unbearable and hopeless suffering.

Jean Kotkin, an AEU Leader and Executive Director of the American Ethical Union indicated that, in her personal judgment, both passive and active euthanasia were permissible under the conditions outlined in the questionnaire. She wrote, "A person must be allowed to die with dignity, not live as a vegetable. We are responsible for ourselves and for our fellow human beings." There is no expressed belief in an afterlife. Indeed, Ms. Kotkin wrote, "If Ethical Culturists go anywhere after they die (which I don't believe), it would be to the library." So far as counseling is concerned, she believes that the aim would be "To try and get them to understand fully the reasons for the act and the consequences for the people left."

Dr. Matthew Ies Spetter, Leader of the Riverdale-Yonkers Society, wrote that involvement in euthanasia would not affect rituals associated with the deceased person because "the dignity of the person is paramount." He stated that in such terminal situations he does "explore the marital relationships deeply before offering any counsel."

Among those who signed "A Plea for Beneficent Euthanasia" were members of the American Humanist Association including Dr. Paul Kurtz, Dr. Sidney Hook, Mary and Lloyd Morain, Bette Chambers and Steward V. Pahl and H. J. Blackham of the British Humanist Association. In 1973 the American Humanist Association formally announced its position on euthanasia in Manifesto II which reads:

> To enhance freedom and dignity the individual must experience a full range of civil liberties in all societies. This includes freedom of speech and the press, political democracy, the legal right of opposition to governmental policies, fair judicial process, religious liberty, freedom of association, and artistic, scientific, and cultural freedom. It also includes a recognition of an individual's right to die with dignity, euthanasia, and the right to suicide.

Sikh Dharma

The headquarters for the Sikh Dharma religion in the U.S.A., Canada, Mexico, Central and South America, Europe, Hong Kong and Australia is located in Los Angeles, California. The Secretary of Religion, Ram Das Kaur Khalsa, responded to the request for information and stated that "No official stand has been taken by Sikh Dharma, which is a world religion of 15 million people. We also have not had any official discussions as such on the topic" (of euthanasia). He commented further:

We believe in keeping our bodies as God has created them, living healthy, happy and holy. We also believe in God's Will, and in being able to accept God's Will, whatever it may be. We do not believe in suicide, as we believe in reincarnation. We do use medicines and believe in surgery when necessary, so the line is very narrow between trying to save a life, and unnecessarily prolonging its stay here on the earth. We are also not afraid of death.

This question would probably be left to the individual to decide, as the individual should have the choice how to live his life.

Hinduism

Swami Swahananda of the Vedanta Society of Southern California writes that there never has been "any official discussion" concerning euthanasia "here or in Ramakrishna Mission in India of which we are a branch." He notes that in Hinduism, in general, "The decision is left to the individual, subject to the laws of the country." He added:

> Recently a very famous incident happened. The well-known Vinobha Bhave, a great disciple of Mahatma Gandhi, and the organizer of the Bhoodan Movement, who became old, stopped taking food. So some newspapers announced. Of course the government did not take any position. Probably it was quietly done.
>   Hinduism doesn't take any dogmatic positions based on theology. In ancient India, that is in very old days, there was occasionally cases of sadhus giving up their life in rivers or mountains. Of course, on very rare occasions.

V. D'Souza, Executive Secretary of the society for the Right to Die With Dignity (India), wrote:

> The classical Hindu tradition is that when a man has served his purpose in life, i.e., performed his functions required of him, brought up his family and has no direct obligations, it is time for him to retire. It is not expected that he should die, but he should retire from life. The term used is 'Sanyas' like the verse:

133

> He's gone to the mountain
> He is lost in the forest
> Like a summer dried fountain
> When our need was the sorest . . .

In other words, the man eclipses himself when he reaches a certain level of spiritual maturity and seeks self-deliverance.

In fact, Jainism, which is a Hindu sect . . . actually demands the most painful form of euthanasia, and such incidents take place time and again. Notable examples in India are a social worker Mr. Gapal Mandlik and Acharya Vinobha Bhave, a respected Gandhian disciple.

Buddhism

Zen Master Serng Sahn wrote regarding the Buddhist position: "Buddha said, 'Don't kill any life.' Many machines and drugs are not necessary. Let all beings live in a natural way. When you die, where do you go?"

Professor H. Uemura of Komazawa University in Tokyo, Japan, wrote concerning the attitude of Zen:

> Dōgen Zenji (1200–1253), who is a famous Buddhist priest wrote about the Life and Death in his writing "Shobogenzo." A literal translation . . . follows: "When the Buddha exists in Life and Death, there is no Life and Death. Also, when the Buddha does not exist in Life and Death, anybody may not be puzzled about Life and Death." I think the meaning in the first half of the sentence is "enlightening," and in the latter is "nothing." . . . The Life and Death is the great natural rule and truth. Of course, this is founded on the Buddhist idea that Life and Death are rotating alternately forever in this world.
>
> So I think that it means that you must endeavour to experience the stage of Buddha, in order to jump over and emancipate from the Life and Death.

Philip Kapleau who edited *The Wheel of Death* (New York: Harper & Row, 1971) quotes the Buddha concerning Karma:

> If you want to know the past (cause), look at your present life (effect). If you want to know the future (effect), look at your present (cause).

135

He records the tale told by Sri Ramana Maharshi concerning Sri Bhagavan (Maharshi) who was offered a palliative to relieve lung congestion, but refused it. He asked to be sat upright. "They knew already that every movement, every touch, was painful, but he told them not to worry about that. He sat with one of the attendants supporting his head. A doctor began to give him oxygen, but with a wave of his hand he motioned him away." He died peacefully shortly after (p. 68).

Kapleau calls attention to the ten precepts of Buddhism, two of which read as follows (pp. 80f): "I resolve not to kill but to cherish all life. I resolve not to cause others to use liquors or drugs which confuse or weaken the mind, nor to do so myself, but to keep my mind clear." He writes:

> No matter where you are in your last hours, insofar as you can control your circumstances, do not allow your mind to be weakened by drugs or other treatments which numb or impair the clarity of your consciousness. If your pain becomes too intense, let your doctor or attendant ease it with drugs which do not render you unconscious.
>
> Your state of mind at the time you draw your last breath is crucial, for upon this hinges your following rebirth.

He recommends that the "heart of Perfect Wisdom" be read to the dying person as part of the terminal care, that the person in attendance seek to calm the mind of the dying person and that all efforts be made to create a serene atmosphere.

George Williams, General Director of the Nichiren Shoshu Soka Gakkai of America, noted that Nichiren Shoshu Buddhism has no official position on euthanasia. He provided an "unofficial viewpoint based on the many concepts of Nichiren Shoshu Buddhism which was expressed in an informal question and answer session." The "summary" he sent is as follows:

> QUESTION: Buddhism expounds the sanctity of life. Suppose a loved one is suffering from unbearable pain and wants to end his life. Is it still against the Buddhist philosophy to allow that person to die?
>
> ANSWER: Your attitude toward euthanasia depends on your definition of "life." If you think a person's life in this world is mere chance, you

will naturally think that you can end the suffering of a loved one by ending his life. And you will regard it as an act of courage and compassion.

It is taught in Buddhism that a human life does not end by physical death but continues to exist throughout eternity, and that its karma, both good and bad, is carried with it into the future. From this, it follows that one's suffering does not end by physical death but that it vanishes only when one changes that karma for the better. Thus Buddhism provides the means to change one's bad karma.

The power to improve one's karma lies in one's own life. It is part of the Buddha nature that is inherent in all life. From the Buddhist viewpoint, all life is infinitely precious because it has the innate Buddha nature or the potential to achieve Buddhahood. The purpose of Buddhist practice is to manifest this Buddha nature or the greatest potential of one's life.

Of course I agree that it is unbearable to see a loved one in extreme pain. In such a condition, that person feels he has no reason to live, so he wants to be allowed to die. The people close to him will think that they should allow his wish to be granted out of their own sense of compassion. But isn't this too materialistic a view of life? Moreover, the truth of life reveals that death is not the final solution to the problem of suffering. The people who cannot bear to see their loved one suffer from pain will be able to stop their own suffering by allowing the person to die, but the karma of suffering still exists within that person's life. The only possible solution is to infuse that person with the life-force to change his own karma for the better. This is why we need Nichiren Daishonin's Buddhism. There is a proverb that says, "Where there is life, there is hope." We should not give up hope as long as we are living. But the hope of being freed from suffering can only be realized when we have strong faith in the Gohonzon.

If people start thinking that they have the right to perform acts of mercy killing, then there is the possibility for this to happen where it can be avoided. It is very easy to accept the idea of euthanasia when many people support it, and it is very difficult to deny it in the face of overwhelming opposition. However, we should find the answer to this problem by understanding what life is, not by mere sympathy.

Krishna

Members of the International Society for Krishna Consciousness, whose followers are often identified as "Hare Krishnas," also believe in karma and reincarnation. These persons find their release from the wheel of life through their Lord Krishna and find guidance in the "timeless Vedic text Bhagavad-gita." In the book *Coming Back: The Science of Reincarnation* (Bhaktivedanta Book Trust, 1982) the editors explain:

> Everything we have thought and done during our life makes an impression on the mind, and the sum total of all these impressions influences our final thoughts at death. According to the quality of these thoughts, material nature awards us a suitable body. Therefore, the type of body that we have now is the expression of our consciousness at the time of our last death (p. 16).

Clearly, the person's state at the moment of death has significance for the next incarnation. Hence, one looks for the perfect example of the way to die. For the members of the Hare Krishna group, that model was provided by Srila Prabhupada, the founder of the organization. According to Satsvarupa Dasa Goswami in *Prabhupada* (Bhaktivedanta Book Trust, 1983), Srila Prabhupada's "departure was exemplary" and "his 'last breathing' was glorious"

> not because of any last-minute mystical demonstration, but because Srila Prabhupada remained in perfect Krishna consciousness. . . . At the time of his departure, therefore, he was teaching how to die, by

138

depending always on Krishna. Prabhupada's passing away was peaceful. During the evening of November 14, the *kaviraja* (an Ayur-Vedic doctor) asked him, "Is there anything you want?" and Prabhupada replied faintly, *Kuch iccha nahi*: "I have no desire." His passing away was in the perfect situation: in Vrndavana (a village that was Krishna's childhood home, but here it means the state of pure Krishna consciousness), with devotees (p. 372).

Although there is no discussion of euthanasia, it is clear that, like the Buddhists, the members of this group prefer to avoid palliatives that might cloud the mind and would reject anything that might alter the natural dying trajectory.

Islam

The leaders of Islam do not seem to have taken any official position concerning the issues of euthanasia, but there is a general understanding that members of the Muslim community are opposed to the practice. At the meeting of the Fifth World Congress of Right-to-Die Societies held in Nice, France in September, 1984, Dr. Mohammed Ali, a Muslim scholar from London, England, explained the basis for Islamic opposition. He stated that, according to Islamic teachings, an individual's moment of death is foreordained: "His birth and his death are already recorded—that is, who will be born and how he is to die." Clearly, euthanasia constitutes an interference with the divine plan.

> Dr. Ali referred to the 17th Surah of the Koran which reads: Glory to Him (Allah) Who carried his servant (Mohammed) by night from the Sacred Mosque (Mecca) to the distant mosque (Jerusalem)—the precincts of which We have blessed—in order that We might show him some of Our sign.

The details of this night journey, known as 'Isra,' have been preserved in the Hadith or "traditions" that are accepted as memories of conversations between the prophet Mohammed and his close followers—or of statements by the prophet, which were at first transmitted orally and finally, some 200 to 300 years after the prophet's death, gathered, edited and recorded. There are two major

Hadiths—that of Abu Abdallah Mohammed al-Bukhari, who died in 870 C.E., and that of Abul-Husain al Muslim, who died in 975. In both traditions, details of the 'Isra' are given.

Having been transported to Jerusalem, the prophet ascended to heaven—a journey known as the Mi'raj—on the back of a beast named al-Buraq, which is described as a white animal, "larger than a donkey, but smaller than a mule" (al-Muslim, LXXV). Then, led by the angel Gabriel, Mohammed passed through the seven heavens.

According to Dr. Ali, it was while Mohammed was in the fourth heaven that he met the angel of death. He asked the angel, "How do you take the life of a person?" The angel replied, "There is a big tree representing all human beings of the universe, with a name written on each one of the leaves. Forty days before the death of a person, the color of the leaf becomes brown, and at the time of the death the leaf will fall to the ground." On the basis of this tradition, Dr. Ali said that euthanasia is "ruled out" in Islam.

My own search of the two Hadiths failed to uncover these details, nor were the librarians at the Center for Islamic Studies in Los Angeles, California able to discover the source. According to al-Muslim, the tree (Sidrat-ul-Muntaha or Lote tree) "whose leaves were like elephant ears and its fruit like big earthenware vessels" is revealed in the seventh heaven. In the seventh heaven, Mohammed did ascend to such heights that he could hear "the scraping of the pens"—presumably of angels recording human destiny. But there is no reference to the withering leaves and human death. The tradition appears in the same form in al-Bukhari.

Inasmuch as there are other collections of Hadiths, perhaps Dr. Ali found the expanded version in one which I failed to consult. What is important for this study is that there is in the interpretation of the Koran and the traditions, a basis for opposition to euthanasia.

Dr. Ali also noted that "pain and suffering . . . are part and parcel of the reduction of sin" in Islamic thought. Clearly, to terminate suffering would interfere with expiation for sin.

The Bahá'ís

Anna Lee Strasburg, responding to the questionnaire on behalf of the Office of the Secretary of the National Spiritual Assembly of the Bahá'ís of the United States, wrote:

The Bahá'í Writings do not contain specific guidance on euthanasia or on the subject of life support systems as used by the medical profession in cases of the terminally ill. Therefore Bahá'ís are free to make their own decisions about the termination of such treatment. The supreme governing body of the Bahá'í Faith considers it untimely to make definitive rulings on certain matters to which no direct reference can be found in the Sacred Text. Rather it is the task of the individual believer to determine, according to his own understanding of the Writings, precisely what his course of conduct should be in relation to situations which he encounters in his daily life.

However, concerning "active" euthanasia or "assisted suicide", the Bahá'í teachings state that suicide is forbidden and that whoever commits suicide endangers his soul and will suffer spiritually in the afterlife.

The manner in which a Bahá'í dies does not affect the application of the Bahá'í burial laws.

General Responses

A number of responses to the questionnaire simply stated that the particular religious group had taken no official position. No hints or suggestions were made as to what the position might be, and no guidelines were provided for understanding the theological basis for arriving at decisions—or an absence of policy.

For example, Floyd D. Carey, Director of Public Relations for the Church of God, wrote, "Our denomination has not taken a position on any of the items you have listed. I regret that we are not able to assist you." Milton A. Tomlinson of the Church of God of Prophecy noted, "We have no teaching on euthanasia. This is a personal matter and is decided by the individual." This same position was reflected in the response from Dr. Rolf K. McPherson, President of the International Church of the Foursquare Gospel. He wrote:

> As a movement, we do not take a stand on such issues, but leave the matter to the pastoral care of a local church and the family involved. The personal convictions of the individual would likely be considered in cases where he/she is capable of making such a decision.

Of course, some churches are autonomous. National organizations hesitate to attempt to make decisions for all participants. Dr. David L. Gray, Dean of the Congregational Foundation for Theological Studies, wrote:

143

> The National Association does not take official stands on behalf of the Congregational Christian Churches since each is autonomous and responsible for their own choices in how to express God's Will for them. I am sure there would be a very wide range of responses within most of our local churches as well as between them. The sacredness of life would probably be commonly held, but what that would mean in actions would undoubtedly differ greatly. We have no particular Committee or source for discussion of this issue at the present time.

There were those who, although no official stand had yet been taken on euthanasia, did suggest that, because positions had been taken on other controversial issues, a similar response might well be expected. For example, Louis L. King, President of the Christian and Missionary Alliance, wrote, "The Christian and Missionary Alliance has not taken an official position on euthanasia. Since, however, our denomination has taken an official anti-abortion stand, I assume our General Council would also vote against euthanasia." Leonard Hoffman, Stated Clerk of the Christian Reformed Church, noted that the denomination had taken stands on "abortion and capital punishment," but had taken no position relative to euthanasia.

Margaret Nix, Media Resource Consultant for the United Church of Canada, consulted with Dr. Howard Brox, Secretary of the Division of Mission in Canada, "under whose department 'euthanasia' would come." She found that: ". . . there has been limited discussion on the subject and there is no specific policy adopted by the General Council. There was some mention of it in the Commission on Ethics and Genetics report at General Council in Calgary in 1977, but nothing definitive."

Similarly, Joseph R. Flower of the Assemblies of God wrote that, "Our church has not officially addressed itself to this issue, but in general our people would be opposed to deliberately terminating life, or doing anything other than saving or preserving it." He provided as scriptural references Psalm 31:15 and Genesis 9:6, noting, "Only God has the right to terminate human life or to decree its termination. So highly does He evaluate it that any human who deliberately takes life will have his life terminated. The reason: man has been made in the image of God."

Neither the National Spiritualist Association, as reported by Elizabeth R. Edgar, Secretary, nor the Society of Friends General Conference, as reported by Lloyd Lee Wilson, General Secretary, have taken a position on euthanasia.

QUESTIONNAIRE

1. What stand or position (if any) has your religious organization taken regarding so-called "passive" euthanasia? By "passive" euthanasia I refer to the removal of life-support systems or the cessation of what have been called "heroic measures" to continue life when the patient is in intractable pain with a terminal illness, or is in irreversible coma, and when the removal of the support system will result in the death of the patient?

   For example: K, 22 years old, is suffering from "a rapidly fulminating type of multiple sclerosis." He has been in a coma for 2 months and does not respond to any attention. He is immobile and body wastes are excreted involuntarily into plastic receptacles. According to his physician, his brain "is gone," his nervous system is rapidly degenerating. He will never recover and, indeed, if it were not for the artificial support system, both heart and breathing would cease to function. (Case drawn from David Hendin: *Death as a Fact of Life,* New York, 1973, pp. 17f.)

   In such a situation would your religious organization sanction the removal of the life-support system and permit K to die? If so: Why and on what ethical and theological grounds? If not: Why not?

2. What stand or position (if any) has your religious organization taken with regard to so-called "active" euthanasia? By "active" euthanasia I refer to the deliberate intervention into the life process by the patient who is terminally ill and in intractable pain, or by the patient acting with the assistance of some other person, or by some person acting on behalf of a patient.

   For example: M is 69 years old and is suffering from a virulent form of cancer that will, according to her doctors, terminate her life within a period of weeks. Her pain is excruciating; and although it is somewhat relieved by drugs, the medications leave her in a semi-comatose state which she resents. She has saved dozens of sleeping pills and other potentially lethal medications which she has hidden away. She knows she is terminal and does not want to live her remaining days in pain and in a semi-comatose state.

In such a situation would your religious organization organization sanction her taking the medication and thereby shorten her time of suffering and end her life, in other words—commit suicide?

Yes _____   No _____

If "yes": Why and on what ethical and theological grounds? If "no": Why not?

Suppose M was not able to collect the lethal medications, but persuaded her doctor or a friend or a relative *to provide her* with the lethal dosage. In such a situation would your religious organization sanction the participation of her associates in her taking of her own life to end suffering? (Assisted suicide)

Yes _____   No _____

If "yes": Why and on what ethical and theological grounds? If "no": Why not?

Suppose the doctor or a friend or relative, acting in accord with M's expressed wishes, *administered* the lethal medications that shortened the time of suffering and caused death. In such a situation would your religious organization sanction this act which can be labeled "homicide" or "murder" or even "compassionate murder"?

Yes _____   No _____

If "yes": Why and on what ethical or theological grounds? If "no": Why not?

3. Does your religious organization espouse belief in a soul or afterlife or in divine judgement or karma? If "yes," circle appropriate terms.

No _____

If "yes": What effect would participation in active euthanasia have upon the afterlife of the deceased and/or the one who participated in the termination of the patient's life?

4. Would the fact that death came by "active" euthanasia affect the rituals or burial patterns of the deceased person? If "yes": How and why? If not: Why not?

5. What sort of counseling would your religious organization provide for someone contemplating "passive" euthanasia for the self or for another (as in the case of K)?

For "active" euthanasia?

6. Will you please provide me with references in Scripture or other religious writings, or to ethical or moral doctrines or statements made by your religious organization or its members pertaining to euthanasia?

7. Are there other persons in your religious organization with whom you think I might communicate for further information about this important subject?

Your name? _____ Organization: _____

Bibliography

Addington, Gordon L. "There May Be No Absolute Answers." *Christianity Today*, 26. (February, 1982), 31.

Arthur, Chris. "Looking at Death." Edinburgh (December 1983).

Ayd, Frank J. Jr. "The Hopeless Case: Medical and Moral Considerations." *The Journal of the American Medical Association*, 181. (September 29, 1962), 83–86.

Bardfeld, Philip A. "Jewish Medical Ethics", *Reconstructionist*. (September, 1976), 7–12.

Bar-Zev, Asher. "Euthanasia: A Classical Ethical Problem in a Modern Context." *Reconstructionist*. (February 1979): 7–10.

Battin, M. Pabst. "The Least Worst Death.", *Hastings Century*, 13. (April 1983): 13–16.

Bayly, Joseph. "Is It Life or Death That is Prolonged?", *Christianity Today*, 26. (February 1982): 30–31.

Bennett, Alistair. "For Scottish Exit.", *Scottish Exit*. (Summer, 1981.)

Blumhagen, Jeanne. "We Cannot Choose in a Moral Vacuum.", *Christianity Today*, 26. (February, 1982): 29–30.

Boeyink, David. "Pain and Suffering.", *The Journal of Religious Ethics*, 2/1. (1974): 85–98.

Byle, Joseph M. Jr. "On Killing and Letting Die." *The New Scholasticism*, 51. (Autumn 1977): 433–452.

Cahill, Lisa Sowle. "A 'Natural Law' Reconsideration of Euthanasia." *The Lincare Quarterly*, 44. (February 1977): 47–63.

Capron, Alexander M. "Death and The Law: A Decade of Change." *Soundings*, 303. (March 1980): 290–320.

Chandler, Russell. "Quinlan Case: The Question-When Is It Time to Die?" *Los Angeles Times*. (November 4, 1975).

Chandler, Russell. 'Rather Die than Take Blood'—Witnesses: New Booklet Explains Sect's Opposition to Transfusions." *Los Angeles Times*. (August 20, 1977).

Chapman, Grace P. "Death for the Dying: Has Anyone the Right to Pull the Plug?" *Christianity Today*, 26. (February 1982): 28–29.

Childress, James F. "Who Shall Live When Not all Can Live?" *Soundings*, 103. (Winter 1970): 239–254.

Childs, James M. Jr. "Euthanasia: An Introduction to a Moral Dilemma." *Currents in Theology and Mission*.

Cooper, Robert M. "Euthanasia and the Notion of 'Death With Dignity.'" *The Christian Century*. (February 21, 1973): 225–227.

Cornell, George W. "Report Condemns Euthanasia: Lutheran Study Calls Issue 'Moral Crucible.'" *Los Angeles Times*. (August 2, 1980).

Cousins, Norman. "The Right to Die." *Saturday Review*. (June 14, 1975): 4.

"The Covenant of Life and the Caring Community." *Church and Society* (July/August 1983): 45–54.

Dagi, Teodoro Forcht. "The Paradox of Euthanasia." *Judaism: A Quarterly Journal* 94. (Spring 1975): 157–167.

Dart, John. "Two Catholics Hit Bishops' Report: Californians Back State 'Right to Die' Law." *Los Angeles Times*.

"Death and Decisions." Excerpts from Papers and Discussion at the *Seventh Annual Euthanasia Conference*, New York, New York. (December 7, 1974) The Euthanasia Educational Council, Inc.

"Death With Dignity OK'D By Methodists" *Los Angeles Times*. (May 7, 1976).

"Dilemmas of Euthanasia." Excerpts from Papers and Discussion at the *Fourth Euthanasia Conference*, New York Academy of Medicine. (December 4, 1971) The Euthanasia Educational Council, Inc.

Dyck, Arthur. "Thou Shalt Not Kill." *Catholic Digest*, 39. (April 1975): 81–84.

Encyclopeida Judaica. "Euthanasia."

Encyclopedia of Bioethics, S.V., "Death and Dying: Euthanasia and Sustaining Life," by Gerald J. Gruman, Sissela Bok and Robert M. Veatch.

Fallows, James. "Entitlements." *The Atlantic Monthly*. (November, 1982): 51–59.

Federbush, Simon. "The Problem of Euthanasia in Jewish Tradition." *Judaism* (January, 1952): 64–68.

Ferber, Max. "'I Cried, Not for Irma, but for the Ignominious Way of Her Going.'" (November 26, 1975).

Gaffney, James. "Fighting for Life: Contest, Sexuality and Consciousness." *New Catholic World*, 224. (May/June, 1981): 139.

Gaffney, James. "The Vatican Declaration on Euthanasia and Some Reflections on Christian Ethical Methodology." *Thought*, 57. (December, 1982): 413–421.

"Gallup Poll Result: Approval of 'Mercy Killing' Rises." *American Medical News*. (August 13, 1973.)

Gaylin, Willard. "Who Should Decide? The Case of Karen Quinlan." *Christianity and Crisis*. (January 19, 1976).

Goodwin, R. Dean. "Thank You, God for Keeping Me Alive." *The American Baptist*. (July-August): 22-23.

Hill, Andrew M. "Another Christian View on Euthanasia." *Scottish Exit Newsletter*. (Spring, 1982).

Holl, Adolf. *Death and The Devil*. (New York, Seabury, 1976): 15ff.

Horowitz, Elliot. "The California Natural Death Act and Us." *Sh'ma*, 15. (April, 1977): 93–102.

"Hospital, Doctors Won't Fight Quinlan Decision." *Los Angeles Times*. (April 9, 1976).

Hyer, Marjorie. "Vatican Eases its Position on Prolonging of Life" *Washington Post*, (June 27, 1980).

"Is Every Life Worth Living?" *Christianity Today*, 26. (March 1982): 12–13.

Jakobowits, Immanuel. *Jewish Medical Ethics*. Philosophical, (New York, 1959).

Jaretzki, Alfred. "Death With Dignity—Passive Euthanasia." *New York State Journal of Medicine*, 76. (April 1976): 539–543.

Kaiser, Robert Blair. "Life and Death Decisions Will Be Made, but By Whom?" New York *Times*. (June 29, 1980).

Kane, T. C. "Suicide." *New Catholic Encyclopedia*.

Kubler-Ross, Elisabeth. *Death: The Final Stage of Growth*. (Prentice-Hall, New Jersey, 1975): 42.

Kung, Hans. "Dying With Christian Dignity." *Commonweal*, 111. (January 1984): 42–43.

Lambert, Tom. "Archbishop's Thoughts on Prolonging Life Praised." *Los Angeles Times*. (December 18, 1976).

Lindrebn, Kris. "Brother of Dead Girl Returned to Parents: Found in Good Health; Sister Died Enroute to Faith Healer." *Los Angeles Times*, (August, 1978).

Mainelli, Vincent P. "Gaudium Et Spes: Pastoral Consitution on the Church in the Modern World." *Social Justice: Official Catholic Teachings.* (McGrath: North Carolina, 1978).

Mainelli, Vincent P. "Message of Pope Paul VI Issued in Union With the Synod of Bishops." *Social Justice: Official Catholic Teachings.* (McGrath: North Carolina, 1978).

Mainelli, Vincent P. "Message of Pope Paul VI for the World Day of Environment." *Social Justice: Official Catholic Teachings.* (McGrath: North Carolina, 1978).

Mainelli, Vincent P. "The Church and Human Rights: Pontifical Commission 'Justitia et Pax'." *Social Justice: Official Catholic Teachings.* (McGrath: North Carolina, 1978).

Manroe, Barbara L. "Ethical and Legal Considerations In Decision-Making For Newborns." *Perkins Journal*, 32. (Summer 1979): 1–9.

McCallum, Gavin. "From a Member of Scottish Exit Committee." *Scottish Exit.* (Spring, 1981).

McCormick, R. A. "Notes on Moral Theology." *Theological Studies*, 37. (April-September 1975): 70–119.

McCormick, Richard A. and Veatch, S. J. Robert. "The Preservation of Life and Self-Determination." *Theological Studies*, 41. (June 1980): 390–396.

McIntyre, Russell L. "Euthanasia: A Soft Paradigm for Medical Ethics." *The Linacre Quarterly*, 45. (February 1978): 41–54.

McNeil, Donald G. Jr. "Brother Joseph and Legal 'Right to Die'." New York *Times.* (November 14, 1979).

Meilaender, Gilbert. "The Distinction between Killing and Allowing to Die." *Theological Studies*, 37. (April-September 1975): 467–477.

Meilaender, Gilbert. "Euthanasia & Christian Vision." *Thought*, 57. (December, 1982): 465–475.

"Missouri Judge Refuses to Order Respirator Off." *Los Angeles Daily Journal.* (October 19, 1975).

"Motion Asks New Guardian for Karen Quinlan" *Los Angeles Daily Journal.* (November 24, 1975).

Neale, Ann. "Bioethical Issues of the Future" *New Catholic World*, 226. (January/February): 40–43.

Neff, H. Richard. "Human Values and Medical Ethics: One Church's Approach." *Health Care Ministries.* (September-October 1977): 42–48.

Paris, John J. "Brother Fox, the Courts and Death With Dignity." *America* (November 8, 1980): 282–285.

Paris, John J. "Death Dilemmas." *The Christian Century*, 98. (March 1981): 253–254.

Parrott, Jennings. "Karen Anne Quinlan." *Los Angeles Times*. (March 29, 1976).

"Patrol Added to Keep Curious Away From Quinlan Girl, Family." *Los Angeles Times*. (April 10, 1976).

Pope John Paul II. "In Love, Faithful to the Truth: Address of Pope John Paul II to the Episcopal Conference of the United States at Quigley Siminary South." *The Pope Speaks*, 24. (Winter 1979): 347–357.

Pope Paul VI. "Pastoral Report on the Holy Year: Address of Pope Paul VI to the Cardinals." *The Pope Speaks*, 20. (Fall 1975): 112–124.

"Quinlan Respirator Decision Appealed." *Los Angeles Daily Journal*. (November 18, 1975).

"Rabbi Urges Change in Euthanasia Ban." *The Los Angeles Times*, (January 26, 1974).

Rachels, James. "Active and Passive Euthanasia." *The New England Journal of Medicine*, (January 9, 1975): 78–80.

Rachels, James. "Active Euthanasia with Parental Consent: Commentary." *Hastings Century*, 9. (October 1979): 19–21.

Ranis, Gustav. "Foreign Aid: Euthanasia or Reform?" *Worldview*. (March 1980): 25–29.

Robertson, John A. "Dilemma in Danville." *Hastings Century*, 11. (October 1981): 5–8.

Sacred Congregation for the Doctrine of the Faith. "Declaration of Euthanasia." New York *Times*, (June 17, 1980).

Schroth, Raymond A. "We Die Before We Live: Talking With the Very Ill." *New Catholic World*, 224. (May/June 1981): 140.

Sellers, James. "Is Euthanasia a Form of Civil Disobedience?" *The Christian Century*, 100. (November 1983): 980.

Seper, Franjo Cardinal and Hamer, Jerome. "Declaration on Euthanasia." *Catholic Mind*. (October 1980): 58–64.

Shannon, Thomas A. "How Brave a New World? Dilemmas in Bioethics." *New Catholic World*, 224. (May/June 1981): 141.

Siegel, Seymour. "A Jewish Approach." *United Synogogue Review*. (Fall 1976): 4–5, 30.

Silving, H. "Euthanasia." *New Catholic Encyclopedia*.

Simmons, Paul D. "Death With Dignity: Christians Confront Euthanasia." *Perspectives in Religious Studies*, 4. (Summer 1977): 141–159.

Simpson, Ean. "Pain or Peace?" *The Right to Die: The Newsletter of Exit*. (Summer, 1980).

Smith, Dana Prom. "Some Thoughts on the 'Quality' of Sacred Life." *Los Angeles Times* (October 24, 1976).

Smolar, Leivy. "The Right to Die, the Bio-Ethical Frontier; Creating an Agenda." *The Journal of Jewish Communal Service*, 103. (Summer 1977): 320–329.

Sobosan, Jeffrey G. "Death: Theological Reflections on a Ministerial Problem." *The Christian Century*. (February 21, 1973): 228–229.

Soper, the Rev., the Lord. "Christian Views on Euthanasia Vary Enormously." *Scottish Exit*. (Autumn 1981).

Scott, John R. W. "What is Human Life Anyway?" *Christianity Today*, 28. (April 1979): 32–33.

Syme, Sonia. "Why do Jewish Kids Ask So Many Questions?" *Keeping Posted*, 24. (March 1979): 22.

Tanner, Henry. "Vatican Reaffirms View on Euthanasia." New York *Times*. (June 17, 1980).

"To Die With Dignity." *Reconstructionist*. (1975): 6.

Unterkefler, Bishop Ernest. "Definition of Death, Living Will Legislation Opposed." *Origins*, 7. (February 1978): 543–544.

Van Buren, Abigail. "Dear Abby: Endorsement for The Living Will." *Los Angeles Times*. (May 6, 197_).

Van Buren, Abigail. "Dear Abby: Living Will—A Legacy to Die." *Los Angeles Times*. (May 6, 197_).

Varga, Andrew. "The Ethics of Infant Euthanasia." *Thought*, 57. (December 1982): 438–448.

Venhuizen, Betty. "A Time to Live, A Time to Die." *The Banner*, 118. (December, 1983): 8–9.

Wennberg, Robert. "Euthanasia: A Sympathetic Appraisal." *Christian Scholars Review*, April 7, 1977): 281–302.

Whale, John. "Helping People to Die: What the Churches Say." London *Sunday Times*. (July 13, 1980).

"When Does a Life End?" *The Economist*. (November 29, 1980): 18.

White, Robert B. "A Demand to Die." *The Hastings Center Report*, 5. (June 1975): 9–10.

Wise, Stephen A. "The Last Word—Whose?" *The Christian Century*, 98. (September 1981): 895–896.

Woodward, Kenneth L. and Mark, Rachel. "Life After Life?" *Newsweek*. (May 1, 1978): 63.

Woodward, Kenneth L. with Gosnell, Mariana. "Living With Dying." *Newsweek*. (May 1, 1978): 52–61.

Other books from The Hemlock Society

(A non-profit educational corporation supporting the option of active voluntary euthanasia for the terminally ill.)

Let Me Die Before I Wake
By Derek Humphry

Discussion and guidance on the problems associated with dignified self-deliverance. Outlines methods of rational suicide.

$10.   Trade distribution by Grove Press
                                                    New York

Jean's Way
By Derek Humphry with Ann Wickett

The true story of one woman's plans to end her own life toward the end of a terminal illness. This book is helpful to other couples in a similar predicament.

$8   Trade distribution by Grove Press
                                                    New York

Commonsense Suicide: The Final Right
By Doris Portwood

A fascinating study of the historical and social background to suicide, the last taboo in our society, especially as it relates to the elderly.

$8.   Trade distribution by Grove Press
                                                    New York

The above books can also be obtained by mail order from the Hemlock Society (PO Box 66218, Los Angeles, CA 90066) by adding $1.50 per title.

Assisted Suicide: The Compassionate Crime

A compilation of famous euthanasia cases from around the world. Invaluable as source material for researchers.

$5 (includes mailing)   Only from The Hemlock Society

Who Believes in Voluntary Euthanasia?

A survey of Hemlock's membership in 1982. Important research data.

$4. (includes mailing)   Only from the Hemlock Society.
                                                    PO Box 66218
                                                    Los Angeles, CA 90066

THE HEMLOCK SOCIETY

A national organization, founded 1980, Los Angeles.
Non-profit, tax deductible 501c3

The Hemlock Society, an educational organization, supports the option of active voluntary euthanasia (self-deliverance) for the advanced terminally ill mature adult, or the seriously incurably physically ill person.

As suicide is no longer a crime, Hemlock believes that assistance in suicide should also be de-criminalized where a terminally ill or seriously incurably ill person requests this help.

If you find yourself in general agreement with the principles, you may wish to join the Hemlock Society for the following reasons:

1. To help the Society's campaign to bring better understanding of euthanasia and to work toward improved laws in this area.
2. To demonstrate through membership that you are in favor of thoughtful, justified, voluntary euthanasia for yourself if it became necessary.
3. To receive the Society's interesting quarterly newsletter, Hemlock Quarterly, to keep you up-to-date with ethical, legal and operating developments. This newsletter is one of the best informed on euthanasia in the world.

❧

Annual membership (January through December)
$20 ($10 after July 1 each year.)

Donations to the Hemlock Society are tax-deductible.

THE HEMLOCK SOCIETY
PO BOX 66218
Los Angeles, CA 90066-0218

Telephone: (213) 391-1871

Designer: Robert S. Tinnon
Composition: Publisher's Typography
Printer: Delta Litho
Binder: Delta Litho
Text: Sabon
Display: Solemnis